DCPL0000473158 (PD)

KU-302-102

BRAINSE DOMHNACH MIDE
DONAGHMEDE LIBRARY
TEL. 8482833

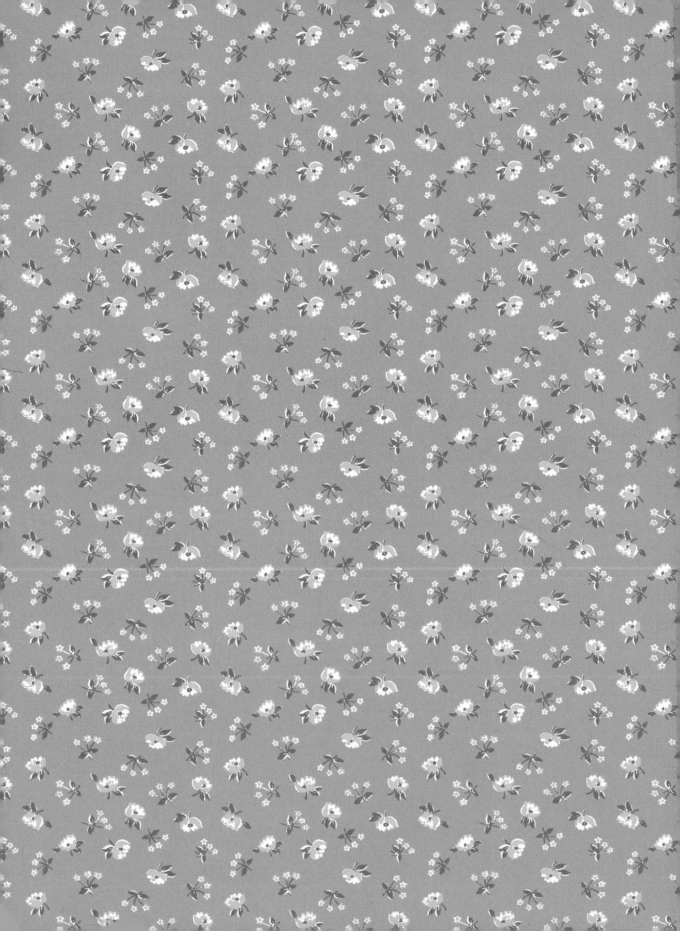

MAKE,
BAKE,
LOVE

MAKE, BAKE, LOVE

*

Lilly Higgins

GILL & MACMILLAN

Gill & Macmillan
Hume Avenue, Park West, Dublin 12
with associated companies throughout the world
www.gillmacmillan.ie

© Lilly Higgins 2011
978 07171 5042 7

Index compiled by Cover to Cover
Design and print origination by Graham Thew
Printed and bound in Italy by L.E.G.O. SpA

This book is typeset in 10pt Neutra on 11pt.

The paper used in this book comes from the wood pulp of managed forests.
For every tree felled, at least one tree is planted, thereby renewing natural
resources.

All rights reserved. No part of this publication may be copied, reproduced or
transmitted in any form or by any means, without permission of the publishers.

A CIP catalogue record for this book is available from the British Library.

5 4 3 2 1

Contents

1 BIG CAKES

2 SMALL CAKES

3 BARS, BISCUITS AND COOKIES

4 PIES AND TARTS

5 BREADS

6 THRIFT

7 MUST-HAVES

x | MAKE, BAKE, LOVE

FOREWORD BY MAEVE HIGGINS

I am delighted that Lilly has created this book because now anyone can learn to bake like her! That is no small feat. If a cake is good enough, people lose their minds. I see this happening time and time again when Lilly bakes. Someone tastes the Boston Cream Cake or catches a glimpse of the Chocolate Peanut Butter Cake and they get a funny look in their eyes. They demand to know who made it. They wonder aloud, what sort of creature is capable of such righteous baking? They try to figure out which cake angel has visited and left a prize for them to eat. Who doesn't want to be the cake angel?

Our mother bakes, a lot. She soaks fruit and softens butter like nobody's business. Lilly inherited our mother's talents for all things cake related and has been baking for a long time. When we were very young, baking was the first job we properly helped with in the kitchen. Cracking eggs, sifting flour and making shapes from pastry were easy for small hands, but now that I'm an adult and a home baker myself, I know that baking is actually quite scientific. Precision really is vital and Lilly is a perfectionist, like our father. She has adjusted and tested her recipes countless times, so you are in safe hands. Follow her instructions carefully and before you know it, you will be a home baker too, with some knock-out cakes in your repertoire!

Lilly's blog, 'Things I Make, Bake and Love', is written in rural Cobh, but read and appreciated online all over the world. People have responded in such lovely ways to Lilly's work so far and I know this book will give many more people great pleasure as well. The food community in Ireland and abroad is wonderfully supportive of what she does and their encouragement and friendship are very important to her.

Each photo in the book has been styled and taken by Lilly, so her personality really does shine through the pages. I admire the finery on show and I know how long it has taken to assemble. Lilly's wonderful collection of beautiful old fabrics, unusually pretty crockery and even wild flowers combine with her gorgeous recipes to create an overall effect that is a tremendous representation of herself and her food.

So, enjoy this book! I hope you will bake as happily as Lilly does.

Maeve Higgins

ACKNOWLEDGEMENTS

I must start by thanking Fergal Tobin, Deirdre Rennison Kunz, Ciara O'Connor, Teresa Daly and all at Gill & Macmillan, as well as the designer, Graham Thew. Their belief in this book as a project has been very encouraging and motivating.

I was extremely lucky to have Kristin Jensen, a talented fellow food blogger (www.dinnerdujour.org) and co-founder of The Irish Food Bloggers Association, to copyedit my text and perfect my vague recipes!

Many thanks to all the teachers and staff at Ballymaloe Cookery School, especially Darina Allen, whose constant enthusiasm for food is infectious. The Ballymaloe food ethos is inspiring and it gave me the confidence to start my blog and cook for as many people as I can.

Thanks to all my lovely blog readers! Sometimes blogging can be a solitary hobby, but your lovely comments and feedback are priceless and very encouraging.

Thanks to all the O'Donovan family, especially Elsie for being a great helper in the kitchen.

Thanks so much to my parents, Dave and Monica, for having an incredible belief in and love for all of their children and for somehow raising all eight of us as individuals!

Massive thanks to my brilliant sisters and brother: Ettie for being so interested in my baking despite all the amazing work she does in Somalia. Oliver for his love of sugar. Maeve for her generous advice and encouragement. Raedi for creating a great running programme for me to work off all the sugar and butter! (www.runlikeagirl.com) Rosie for her daily support and amazing make-up artistry skills. Daisy for her enthusiasm and willingness to try everything I made. Last but not least, Aggy for supplying me with hens' eggs, just when I needed them!

And finally, thanks to Colm: love of my life, light of my eye and boy that makes my heart go boom.

Lilly Higgins

July 2011

Conversion Charts

Weight

30g	1oz
60g	2oz
90g	3oz
110g	4oz
140g	5oz
170g	6oz
200g	7oz
225g	8oz
250g	9oz
280g	10oz
310g	11oz
340g	12oz
370g	13oz
400g	14oz
425g	15oz
450g	1lb
500g	18oz
570g	1 1/4lb
680g	1 1/2lb
900g	2lb
1kg	2 1/4lb
1.1kg	2 1/2lb
1.4kg	3lb
1.5 kg	3lb 5oz
1.8kg	4lb
2kg	4 1/2lb
2.2kg	5lb

Volume

5ml	1 teaspoon
10ml	1 dessertspoon
15ml	1 tablespoon
30ml	1 fl oz
60ml	2 fl oz
90ml	3 fl oz
120ml	4 fl oz
150ml	5 fl oz
175ml	6 fl oz
200ml	7 fl oz
240ml	8 fl oz
270ml	9 fl oz
300ml	10 fl oz
325ml	11 fl oz
350ml	12 fl oz
400ml	14 fl oz
450ml	15 fl oz
475ml	16 fl oz
1 litre	34 fl oz

Oven

Degrees Celsius	Degrees Fahrenheit	Gas Mark	Description
140	275	1	Very cool
150	300	2	Cool
160	325	3	Warm
180	350	4	Moderate
190	375	5	Fairly hot
200	400	6	Fairly hot
220	425	7	Hot
230	450	8	Very hot
240	475	9	Very hot

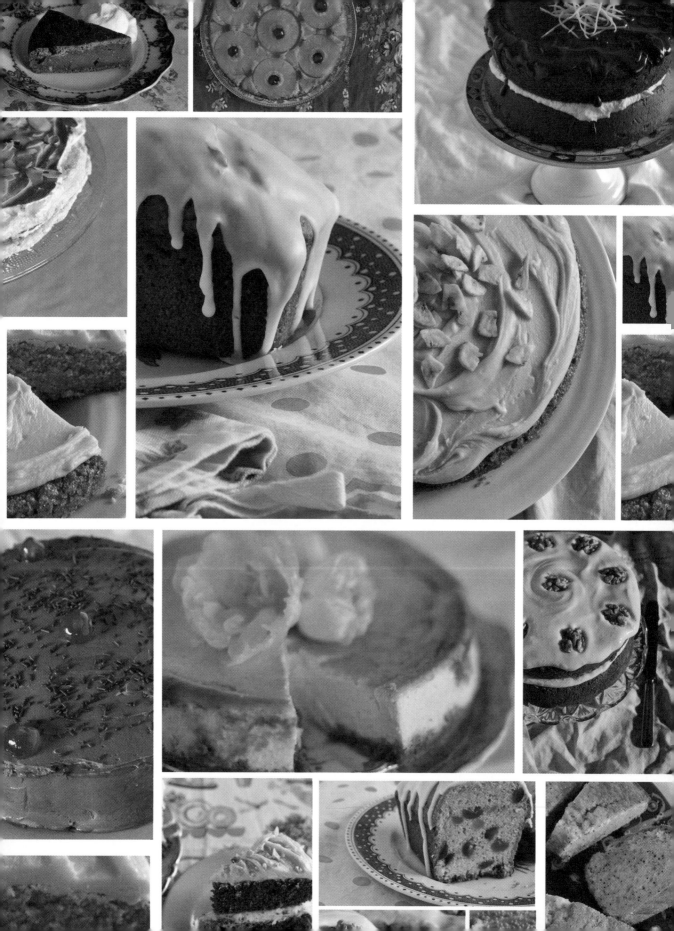

CHAPTER 1

Big Cakes

BANOFFEE CAKE

SERVES 10-12

....

This butterless banana cake is perfectly moist and beautifully balanced with the toffee icing. If you don't want lashings of toffee gorgeousness atop your cake, then just butter the sides of the tin and coat in Demerara sugar for a crunchy, sweet coating on the cake's edges.

FOR THE CAKE:
225g plain flour
1 tsp baking powder
3 eggs
170g Demerara sugar
2 medium ripe bananas, mashed
1 tsp vanilla essence
225ml olive oil

FOR THE TOFFEE ICING:
220g Demerara sugar
60g butter
60ml milk
240g icing sugar, sieved
½ tsp vanilla essence

banana chips, to decorate

1 Preheat the oven to 180°C. Butter a 28cm springform tin and dust with flour or Demerara sugar (see note above).

2 Sieve the flour and baking powder into a bowl. Set aside.

3 In a separate bowl, beat the eggs and sugar on high with an electric mixer until thickened and light in colour. Fold in the mashed banana and vanilla. Slowly drizzle in the olive oil while still mixing.

4 Add the flour mixture and mix on low speed, taking care not to overmix. Pour the batter into the prepared tin.

5 Bake for 25-30 minutes, until golden. Cool fully on a rack before icing.

6 To make the icing, place the sugar, butter and milk into a pan over a high heat. Stir everything well and bring to the boil. Keep stirring and boil for 1 minute.

7 Remove from the heat and beat in half of the icing sugar. Allow to cool slightly, then add the vanilla and the rest of the sugar. Beat well until it thickens.

8 Spread the icing over the cake straightaway, as the icing will harden slightly. Top with banana chips.

Leabharlanna Poibli Chathair Bhaile Átha Cliath
Dublin City Public Libraries

BAKED VANILLA CHEESECAKE

SERVES 8–10

I absolutely love cheesecake and baked vanilla has to be my favourite. This version has ricotta in it, so it's not too sickly sweet or smooth. This cake keeps really well in the fridge for a few days but is nicest the day it's made. I sometimes use half Ginger Nuts for the base and add a pinch of ground ginger to the filling. Or you could use chocolate digestives and add the zest of a lime and lime juice instead of lemon. It's also really nice with sugared strawberries piled on the top just before serving. A really handy recipe to have up your sleeve!

200g digestive biscuits, crushed
70g butter, melted
5 eggs
500g ricotta
500g cream cheese
130g icing sugar, sieved
1 tbsp plain flour
200ml cream
juice of 2 lemons
1 tsp vanilla essence

1. Preheat the oven to 180°C. Butter a 20cm springform cake tin. Line the base and sides with parchment paper.
2. Combine the crushed biscuits with the melted butter in a bowl, then press the mixture evenly over the base of the tin.
3. Mix the cheeses, sugar, flour, cream, lemon juice and vanilla in a large bowl until smooth. Pour the batter over the base in the tin. Bake for 45 minutes, or until just set.
4. Remove from the oven and leave to cool in the tin.

BLACK FOREST GATEAU

SERVES 8–10

My boyfriend Colm's favourite cake is a Black Forest Gateau. A few years ago I made a massive towering cake with six layers in order to impress/spoil him for his birthday. Needless to say, it was impossible to cut, but it was gorgeous and he was impressed, so job done there! If you love the idea of this classic cake but don't want to make a massive one, then why not start by making the Mini Black Forest Cakes on p. 56?

I was given a bottle of kirsch full of black cherries recently by a Polish friend. She had brought it back from Poland with her, but it can be bought in some Polish shops here in Ireland too. The cherries were soaked right through with the glorious alcohol. They were amazing folded into pancakes and stirred through Greek yoghurt. Come to think of it, actually, everything is better when these beauties are added!

225g butter, softened
225g caster sugar
4 eggs
225g self-raising flour
3 tbsp cocoa powder, plus extra to decorate
50ml milk
1 x 425g tin of black cherries, drained, or 220g fresh/frozen cherries
100ml kirsch (cherry liquor)
300ml cream, whipped
fresh cherries, to decorate

1 Preheat the oven to 180°C. Butter and flour 2 x 20cm sandwich cake tins.

2 Cream the butter and sugar together in a bowl until light and fluffy. Add the eggs one by one, mixing well after each addition.

3 Sieve the flour and cocoa into the bowl, add the milk and mix until just combined. Fold in the cherries, taking care not to overmix. Divide the batter between the 2 tins.

4 Bake for 25–30 minutes, until an inserted skewer comes out clean. Leave to cool in the tin for a few minutes before turning out onto a rack to cool fully.

5 Slice the cakes in half horizontally. Sprinkle one-third of the kirsch over one layer of cake. Top with whipped cream, another layer of cake, kirsch, etc. Finish with the final layer of cake, a swirl of whipped cream and fresh cherries and dust with cocoa.

BOSTON CREAM CAKE

SERVES 8–10

My great-grandmother Lillian Archdeacon (whom I'm named after – the Lillian bit) lived in Boston for a few years. She loved to cook and bake and brought lots of new and exciting recipes back to Ireland with her. This is one of her recipes that I found tucked into her recipe book. It's handwritten and dated 12 December 1912. I've made this cake a few times and learned the hard way that 5 teaspoons of baking powder does not a good cake make! Baking powder has come a long way since 1912, but I wanted to try it to her exact recipe first. Her cake was left uniced, but I've added the traditional Boston cake filling and chocolate ganache. A very special cake.

FOR THE CAKE:
300g caster sugar
150g butter, softened
4 eggs
1 tsp vanilla essence
400g self-raising flour
1 tsp baking powder
250ml milk

FOR THE GANACHE:
100g dark chocolate
40g butter

FOR THE CUSTARD FILLING:
55g caster sugar
30g custard powder
170ml milk
120ml cream, divided
1 tsp vanilla essence

1 Preheat the oven to 180°C. Butter and flour 2 x 20cm sandwich tins.

2 To make the cake, cream the sugar and butter together in a bowl until light and fluffy. Add the eggs one by one, mixing well after each addition. Add the vanilla and mix.

3 Sieve the flour and baking powder together in a bowl. Add to the butter and sugar mixture, alternating with the milk, until everything is well combined. Pour the batter into the prepared tins and bake for 40 minutes, until golden and an inserted skewer comes out clean.

4 To make the custard filling, combine the sugar and custard powder in a small saucepan over a medium heat so it doesn't boil over. Gradually stir in the milk and 50ml cream. Stir until the mixture thickens and boils. Remove from the heat and stir in the vanilla. Cover the top of the custard directly with cling film and leave to cool. Meanwhile, whip the remaining 70ml cream. Once the custard has cooled, fold in the whipped cream.

5 To make the ganache, melt the chocolate with the butter in a heatproof bowl over a pan of simmering water. Remove from the heat and stir well until the mixture thickens.

6 To assemble the cake, place one cake on a serving plate and generously spread with the custard filling. Gently top with the remaining cake and pour over the chocolate ganache. Beautiful!

CARROT CAKE

SERVES 8–10

This is *the* carrot cake to make. It's lightly spiced, moist, fluffy and just sweet enough. I've been looking for a really nice carrot cake recipe and even wrote to a café whose cake I tasted and loved. I couldn't figure out what the key ingredient was. They wrote back saying that they wouldn't tell me (gasp! I know!) and that their recipe is a closely guarded family secret. Well, I went back there, ordered a pot of tea, ate a load more of their carrot cake and bingo! I discovered the secret ingredient: pineapple!

Preparing this cake is a lot easier if you have a food processor with a grating attachment for the carrot - it'll take no time!

FOR THE CAKE:
180g Demerara sugar
225ml sunflower oil
3 eggs
½ tsp vanilla essence
300g self-raising flour
2 tsp ground ginger
1 tsp ground cinnamon
1 tsp baking powder
½ tsp bread soda
300g carrots, peeled and coarsely grated
250g tinned pineapple, chopped
50g walnuts, toasted and chopped

FOR THE ICING:
150g icing sugar, sieved
50g butter, softened
400g cream cheese, cold
zest and juice of 1 lime

toasted walnut halves, to decorate

1 Preheat the oven to 180°C. Butter and flour 2 x 20cm sandwich tins.

2 Beat the sugar, oil, eggs and vanilla in a bowl until creamy.

3 In a separate bowl, sieve the flour, spices, baking powder and bread soda together, then fold into the egg mixture. Gently fold in the carrots, pineapple and nuts.

4 Pour the batter into the prepared tins and bake for 35–40 minutes, until an inserted skewer comes out clean. Cool fully on a wire rack.

5 To make the icing, beat the sugar and butter until well combined. Add the cream cheese and beat until just combined. (Be careful not to overbeat the cream cheese or the icing will be too runny.) Add the lime zest and juice and mix gently.

6 To assemble the cake, place one cake on a serving plate and spread half the icing over the top. Top with the second cake and the remaining icing. Stud with toasted walnuts to decorate.

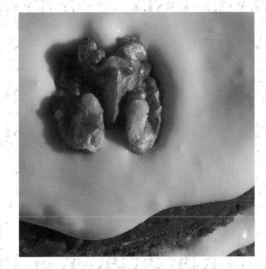

CHOCOLATE FUDGE CAKE

SERVES 8-10

This is a real 1980s birthday cake. It's a great basic cake mix that can be tailored for any occasion. You could crush Flakes over the top, pile chopped Mars bars or mini Easter eggs in the middle or fold a handful of raspberries into the batter before sandwiching the layers with raspberry conserve (or good old jam like we had in the 80s!).

125g dark chocolate, chopped
200g Demerara sugar
180g butter, softened
3 eggs
180g plain flour
1 tsp baking powder
225ml natural yoghurt
1 tsp vanilla essence
chocolate buttercream (double the recipe on p. 194)
glacé cherries, to decorate

1 Preheat the oven to 180°C. Butter and flour 2 x 20cm sandwich tins.
2 Melt the chocolate in a heatproof bowl over a pan of simmering water. Leave to cool slightly.
3 Beat the sugar and butter in a separate bowl until light and fluffy. Add the eggs one at a time, mixing well after each addition.
4 Sieve the flour and baking powder into the bowl. Mix gently. Add the yoghurt, vanilla and the melted chocolate. Fold in gently with a metal spoon or spatula.
5 Divide the batter evenly between the tins and make a slight hollow in the centre so they rise evenly.
6 Bake for 25-30 minutes, until an inserted skewer comes out clean. Leave to cool on a rack and sandwich together with half of the chocolate buttercream. Spread the remaining buttercream on top and stud with cherries or decorations of your choice (see note above).

CHOCOLATE PEANUT BUTTER CAKE

SERVES 8–10

Oh, cake of cakes! Peanut butter and chocolate is a winning combination. Covering the inside of the tins with chopped nuts adds a lovely texture and flavour, but you can just use flour if you like. To go totally overboard, you could pile some mini chocolate peanut butter drops or chocolate-covered nuts on top. A salty-sweet dream cake!

FOR THE CAKE:
60g dry-roasted peanuts, chopped, plus extra to decorate
225g butter, softened
225g caster sugar
4 eggs
100ml milk
225g self-raising flour
3 tbsp cocoa powder
2 tsp baking powder

FOR THE PEANUT BUTTER CREAM:
250g icing sugar, sieved
125g smooth peanut butter
30g butter, softened
50ml milk
1 tsp vanilla essence

1. Preheat the oven to 180°C. Butter 2 x 20cm sandwich tins and cover with the chopped nuts.
2. Cream the butter and sugar together in a bowl until light and fluffy. Add the eggs one by one, mixing well after each addition. Mix in the milk.
3. Sieve the flour, cocoa and baking powder into the egg mixture. Mix until just combined, taking care not to overmix.
4. Spoon the batter into the prepared sandwich tins, taking care not to disturb the nuts. Bake for 30 minutes, until an inserted skewer comes out clean. Allow to cool fully on a rack.
5. To make the icing, cream together half the icing sugar, the peanut butter, butter, milk and vanilla in a bowl until well combined. Add the rest of the icing sugar and mix well, until fluffy.
6. Sandwich the cake together with some icing. Top with more icing and roasted peanuts.

CHOCOLATE ORANGE CAKE

SERVES 8–10

This is the ultimate jaffa cake for the chocolate orange lover in your life! It really is worth using good-quality chocolate for the ganache and I think Green & Blacks Maya Gold is perfect, as it not only has a fresh orange flavour, but it also has a lovely spicy warmth. You could also decorate the top of this cake with slices of chocolate orange or candied orange slices.

FOR THE CAKE:
225g butter, softened
225g caster sugar
4 eggs
50ml milk
juice of 1 orange
225g self-raising flour
3 tbsp cocoa powder
2 tsp baking powder

FOR THE GANACHE:
100g orange dark chocolate (such as Green & Blacks Maya Gold), chopped
40g butter

FOR THE ORANGE ICING:
250g icing sugar, sieved
55g butter, softened
3 tbsp orange juice
1 tbsp milk

thinly sliced rind of ½ orange, to decorate

1 Preheat the oven to 180°C. Butter 2 x 20cm sandwich tins and dust lightly with flour.

2 Cream the butter and sugar together in a bowl until light and fluffy. Add the eggs one by one, mixing well after each addition. Mix in the milk and orange juice.

3 Sieve the flour, cocoa and baking powder into the egg mixture. Mix until just combined.

4 Spoon the mixture into the prepared sandwich tins. Bake for 30 minutes, until an inserted skewer comes out clean. Cool fully on a rack.

5 To make the icing, mix half of the icing sugar, the butter, orange juice and milk until well combined. Add the rest of the icing sugar and mix well, until fluffy. Sandwich the fully cooled cakes together with the icing.

6 To make the ganache, place the chocolate and butter into a heatproof bowl set over a pan of simmering water. Stir until melted. Leave to cool slightly and thicken before spreading generously over the top of the cake. Decorate the top with the orange rind.

COFFEE CAKE

SERVES 8–10

There's nothing like coffee cake. A slice of this with a cup of coffee is absolutely gorgeous and inexplicably nostalgic (even though I never ate it as a child!). It's very easy to make – if you're going to bake a cake for someone as a present, then this is the one! I usually make a strong espresso from the coffee machine and use that for the cake and icing, but granules or coffee essence work perfectly too.

FOR THE CAKE:
180g butter, softened
100g caster sugar
80g Demerara sugar
3 eggs
180g plain flour
1 tsp baking powder
2 tbsp espresso or strong coffee

FOR THE ICING:
350g icing sugar, sieved
150g butter, softened
2 tbsp espresso or strong coffee

200g flaked almonds, toasted, to decorate

1. Preheat the oven to 180°C. Butter and flour 2 x 20cm sandwich cake tins.
2. Cream the butter and sugar together in a bowl until light and fluffy. Add the eggs one by one, mixing well after each addition.
3. Sieve the flour and baking powder together in a bowl, then fold into the egg mixture. Mix in the coffee until everything is just combined.
4. Divide the batter between the tins. Bake for 25–30 minutes, until an inserted skewer comes out clean. Leave to cool in the tins for a few minutes before turning out onto a rack to cool fully.
5. To make the icing, cream the sugar and butter together in a bowl until fluffy. Add the coffee and mix until well combined.
6. Place one cake on a serving plate and cover with icing. Top with the second cake and cover the whole cake, top and sides, with a thin layer of icing. This is your crumb layer – it is used as a base layer of icing and you can then spread more icing over this layer, so don't worry if some crumbs get mixed up in the icing.
7. Fill a piping bag with the remaining icing and use to decorate the cake, or just spread the icing generously all over the cake with an offset spatula. Carefully cover the sides with the flaked and toasted almonds.

SWAN MERINGUE

SERVES 12–15

Swans always look like they're made out of meringue, floating majestically. I made small individual swans for my boyfriend for Valentine's Day, and let me tell you, nothing impresses a boy more than shaped sugar birds. Be careful assembling the swan and take your time at every stage in case you break something. It does stay put for a few hours, but it's safest to assemble at the last minute.

6 egg whites
375g icing sugar, sieved
400ml cream
blueberries or strawberries, to decorate

1. Preheat the oven to 150°C. Line 2 large baking trays with parchment paper. Draw a neck, 2 wings and a base for the swan onto the parchment paper. Flip over the paper so you don't get pencil marks on the meringue.

2. Whisk the egg whites and icing sugar until the mixture is glossy and forms stiff peaks. Fill a piping bag fitted with a plain medium-sized nozzle. Carefully pipe the neck, head and wings following the template on the parchment paper. You can use a spoon to spread the meringue onto the main body template.

3. Bake in the oven for 45–60 minutes, until the meringue lifts off the paper easily. Turn the oven off and leave the meringue in the oven to cool fully with the oven door ajar.

4. Once fully cooled and just before serving, whip the cream. Cover most of the base with whipped cream. Stick the wings and neck in place and cover the cream with berries.

COFFEE MERINGUE CAKE

SERVES 10–12

This is like a large macaroon cake. It's gorgeous with fresh coffee.

FOR THE MERINGUE:
4 egg whites
150g icing sugar, sieved
75g ground almonds

FOR THE BUTTERCREAM:
4 egg yolks
125g icing sugar, sieved
2 tbsp strong coffee or coffee essence
125g butter, softened

a handful of flaked almonds, toasted, to decorate

1 Preheat the oven to 130°C. Line 2 baking trays with parchment paper. Draw 2 circles of the same size onto each piece of parchment. Flip over the paper so you don't get pencil marks on the meringue.

2 In a spotlessly clean, dry bowl, whisk the egg whites until they form stiff peaks.

3 Meanwhile, sieve the icing sugar and ground almonds. Gently fold into the egg whites with a metal spoon or spatula. Divide the meringue mixture evenly between the 2 baking trays and spread into a circle, using your template.

4 Bake for about 1 hour, until the meringue lifts easily from the paper. Turn off the oven and leave the meringue in the oven to cool fully with the door ajar before lifting from the trays onto a serving plate.

5 To make the buttercream, put the egg yolks and icing sugar in a heatproof bowl over a pan of simmering water. Whisk until light and fluffy. Add the coffee essence and continue to whisk until thick and foamy. Remove from the heat and leave to cool. Once cooled, beat in the butter a little at a time.

6 Sandwich the meringues together using this buttercream. Spread half in the centre and half on top. Scatter toasted almond flakes on top to decorate.

DUCK EGG SPONGE

SERVES 8–10

Duck eggs are miraculous! When you whisk them with sugar, a voluminous mousse appears. They're great for baking and give this sponge a gorgeous flavour. You can use 6 hen's eggs in this recipe if you can't find duck eggs.

4 duck eggs (or 6 hen's eggs)
215g caster sugar
170g plain flour, sieved
50g strawberry jam
100g strawberries, sliced
200ml cream, whipped
icing sugar, to decorate

1. Preheat the oven to 180°C. Butter and flour 2 x 20cm sandwich tins.
2. Beat the eggs and sugar together in a bowl until very thick and pale. Carefully fold in the sieved flour.
3. Pour the batter into the prepared tins and bake for 25–30 minutes, until the sponge springs back when pressed and an inserted skewer comes out clean. Allow the cake to sit in the tin for 5 minutes before turning out onto a rack to cool.
4. Place one cake on a serving plate and spread with the strawberry jam and strawberry slices. Top with the whipped cream, then top with the second cake. Dust with icing sugar to decorate.

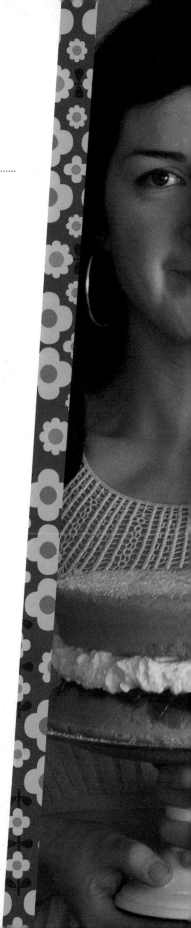

FIG CAKE

SERVES 15–20

This cake keeps really well for over a week. The warm, sweet vanilla works beautifully in it. It's gorgeous for breakfast with strong tea or for dessert with Greek yoghurt. It's dense and packed full of figgy energy – a great cake for the triathlete in your life!

225g dried figs
1 tsp bread soda
150ml buttermilk
285g plain flour
1 tsp baking powder
1 tsp mixed spice
170g caster sugar
110g butter, softened
2 eggs
1 tsp vanilla essence

1 Preheat the oven to 180°C. Butter and flour a 22cm springform tin.

2 Place the figs in a medium saucepan and cover with water. Simmer over a low heat until soft. Drain the figs into a sieve over a bowl and keep the figgy water.

3 Add the bread soda to the softened figs. Blitz the mixture with a hand-held blender or in a food processor until quite smooth. Set aside.

4 Mix 150ml of the figgy water with the buttermilk.

5 Sieve the flour, baking powder and mixed spice into a bowl.

6 Cream the sugar and butter together in another bowl until light and fluffy. Add in the eggs one at a time, mixing well after each addition. Add the flour and the buttermilk mixture and mix gently. Add the vanilla and the fig purée and mix until just combined.

7 Pour the batter into the prepared tin and bake for 45–60 minutes, until an inserted skewer comes out clean and the cake shrinks away from the side of the tin. Allow to sit in the tin for 5 minutes before releasing the sides of the springform tin.

HONEY CAKE

SERVES 10-12

This is a dense butterless cake that keeps well in a tin for a few days. It's slightly sweet with a lovely honey-tinged nuttiness.

100g Demerara sugar
200ml Greek yoghurt
200g ground almonds
100g honey
1 egg, separated
175g plain flour
2 tsp baking powder

1 Preheat the oven to 170°C. Butter and flour a 25cm cake tin or a 25cm ring mould tin.

2 Whisk the sugar and yoghurt together. Stir in the ground almonds, honey and egg yolk. Sieve in the flour and baking powder and mix until just combined.

3 In a spotlessly clean, dry bowl, beat the egg white until it forms soft peaks. Fold into the cake mix.

4 Spoon the batter into the cake tin and bake for 40-45 minutes. Leave to rest in the tin for 5-10 minutes before turning out onto a wire rack to cool.

LEMON POPPY SEED CAKE

SERVES 10–12

This is one of those brilliant oil-based, butter-free cake mixes. If you would love something simple and guaranteed to taste great, then this is the cake for you! You can also change the mix: try using raspberry yoghurt and a handful of frozen raspberries, blueberries, blackberries and a grated apple. I love using a ring mould tin, as the resulting cake is easy to slice and great for a big group.

250g plain flour, sieved
250g caster sugar
150ml natural yoghurt
150ml sunflower oil
3 eggs
zest of 1 lemon
1 tbsp poppy seeds

1   Preheat the oven to 180°C. Butter and flour a 20cm round cake tin or a ring mould.
2   Mix everything together in a large bowl till smooth. Pour the batter into the prepared tin.
3   Bake for 30–40 minutes, until firm to the touch. Allow to cool slightly in the tin before turning out onto a wire rack.

PINEAPPLE UPSIDE-DOWN CAKE

SERVES 10–12

This is one of the first cakes I ever made. On Sundays we would always do loads of baking, and squash the tarts and sponges into the oven alongside the roast chicken and potatoes! Sundays always meant lots of people in the kitchen, lots of washing up and lots of lovely food. You really need the ruby red glacé cherries for this!

Demerara sugar, for the tin
250g caster sugar
200g butter, very soft
3 eggs
250g plain flour
2 tbsp baking powder
6 tbsp pineapple juice (from the tin is fine)
1 x 250g tin pineapple rings
handful of glacé cherries

1 Preheat the oven to 180°C. Butter and dust a 20cm springform tin with Demerara sugar.
2 Cream the sugar and butter together in a large bowl. Add the eggs one by one, mixing well after each addition.
3 Sieve the flour and baking powder into a bowl, then gradually add to the egg mixture, alternating with the pineapple juice. Mix until smooth.
4 Arrange the pineapple rings on the base of the cake tin and stud with the cherries. Top with the batter and smooth over. Bake for 45–50 minutes, until golden and an inserted skewer comes out clean.
5 Leave in the tin to cool slightly, then carefully turn upside down onto a serving plate.

RHUBARB AND CUSTARD CAKE

SERVES 10–12

I think this might be my favourite cake, although I feel bad for the other cakes when I say that. My mother always insists that of her eight children she doesn't have one particular favourite – we're all her favourite in different ways, etc. So diplomatic, but I suppose you have to be with seven daughters! Adopting her diplomacy, I'll say that this is my most favourite Rhubarb and Custard Cake. I dreamt this cake up one day when I was given loads of rhubarb from my father's garden and wanted to make something special for him. I've also baked this cake in a large ceramic tart dish and served it as a sponge with whipped cream. It tastes gorgeous and is even better the following day.

FOR THE CAKE:
240g caster sugar
225g butter, softened
3 eggs
50ml milk
1 tsp vanilla essence
200g self-raising flour
35g custard powder
1 tsp baking powder
300g pink rhubarb, chopped
 into medium chunks

FOR THE ICING:
80g butter, softened
450g icing sugar, sieved
60g custard powder, sieved
50ml milk
1 tsp vanilla essence

hundreds and thousands, to decorate

1 Preheat the oven to 180°C. Butter and flour 2 x 20cm sandwich tins.

2 Cream the sugar and butter together in a bowl until light and fluffy. Add the eggs one by one, mixing well after each addition. Add the milk and vanilla and mix until well combined.

3 Sieve the flour, custard powder and baking powder into the egg mix. Carefully fold in the dry ingredients. Tumble in the rhubarb and give it a final stir.

4 Spoon the batter into the prepared tins and bake for 25–30 minutes, until an inserted skewer comes out clean. Leave to rest in the tin for a few minutes before turning onto a rack to cool.

5 To make the icing, cream the butter with half the sugar. Add the custard powder, milk and vanilla and the remaining icing sugar. Mix until well combined.

6 Place one cake on a serving plate and spread the top generously with icing. Sandwich the cakes together and top with more of the icing. Sprinkle with hundreds and thousands to decorate.

RED VELVET CAKE

SERVES 10-12

Red Velvet Cake is enjoying a bit of popularity at the moment. It's a very striking cake and also quick and easy to make. You'll need three sandwich tins for this giant cake and a whole 25ml bottle of food dye! It's a cute idea too to swap the red food dye for green on St Patrick's Day and omit the cocoa. You could even do one green, one white and one orange layer, both patriotic and delicious!

FOR THE CAKE:
280g self-raising flour
2 tbsp cocoa powder
1 tsp bread soda
340g caster sugar
2 eggs
350ml vegetable oil
250ml buttermilk
1 tsp vanilla essence
25ml (2 ½ tbsp) red food dye
½ tsp white wine vinegar

FOR THE CREAM CHEESE ICING:
100g butter, softened
600g icing sugar, sieved
250g cream cheese, cold
1 tsp vanilla essence

1. Preheat the oven to 180°C. Butter and flour 3 x 20cm sandwich tins.

2. Sieve the flour, cocoa and bread soda together into a large bowl. Stir in the sugar.

3. Whisk the eggs in a large jug. Add the oil, buttermilk and vanilla and mix well. Add the red food dye for dramatic effect and the vinegar. Carefully fold into the dry ingredients.

4. Divide the coloured batter evenly between the tins. Make a little hollow in the centre of each so they will rise evenly. Bake for 25-30 minutes, until an inserted skewer comes out clean and the cake springs back when pressed. Leave to rest in the tins for 5 minutes before turning out onto a wire rack to cool.

5. To make the icing, cream the butter with half the icing sugar in a bowl until well combined. Add the cold cream cheese, vanilla and remaining sugar. Only mix as much as you have to in order to combine the ingredients, as the cream cheese will melt the more you beat it and make your icing runny.

6. To assemble the cooled cake, lightly dust any loose crumbs off the cakes and keep the crumbs to one side. Place one cake on a serving plate and cover with icing. Top with the second cake and cover that with icing, then top with the third cake.

7 Use a small amount of icing to cover the entire cake. It's OK if some of the crumbs combine with the icing – this is meant to happen, as this is the crumb layer (the base layer of icing that ensures the remaining icing goes on cleanly). Leave to set for 10 minutes in a cold place.

8 Using a clean butter knife or offset spatula, resume icing the cake by generously spreading the remaining icing all over the crumb layer. Sprinkle the top with the reserved red cake crumbs to give a hint of what's inside!

SWISS ROLL (GLUTEN FREE)

SERVES 8–10

This gorgeous Swiss roll is really easy to make and nobody would guess it's gluten free. It's the quickest cake ever to bake! It also makes a great base for the trifle on p. 172 if you want to make it coeliac friendly.

Xanthan powder, gluten-free baking powder and all the alternative flours are available in most shops now or else in health food shops.

4 eggs, separated
100g caster sugar, plus extra to decorate
65g rice flour
65g potato flour
1 tsp baking powder
½ tsp xanthan gum
6 tbsp strawberry jam

1   Preheat the oven to 190°C. Butter and line a 20cm x 30cm Swiss roll tin with greaseproof paper.
2   Whisk the egg yolks and sugar in a large bowl until pale yellow.
3   Sieve the rice and potato flours, baking powder and xanthan gum into the bowl. Using a spatula or metal spoon, fold the flour mixture gently into the egg mousse.
4   In a spotlessly clean, dry bowl, whip the egg whites at high speed until stiff peaks form.
5   Fold half the egg whites into the egg and flour mixture to loosen it up. Add the remaining egg whites and fold until well combined.
6   Spread the batter onto the prepared tin. Bake for 8–10 minutes, until golden brown.
7   Leave to cool in the tin for 5 minutes. Place some parchment paper onto your work surface and dust with sugar.
8   Flip the cake out onto the paper and peel the lining paper off of the top of the cake.
9   Using the bottom sheet of paper, gently start to roll the cake onto itself using the longest edge. Leave to cool completely, then unroll, fill with jam and reroll. Dust with more sugar if needed. Serve straightaway.

MARBLE CAKE

SERVES 8–10

Marble Cake is the type of thing that makes kids have tantrums in shops. They really want – no, need – the cake that is somehow magically divided into different colours. Marble Cake is the best of the multicoloured bunch: Neapolitan ice cream isn't nice, Battenberg looks great but tastes horrible and that bear-shaped luncheon roll in the supermarket is dreadful! This cake keeps really well, but if you have any left over, then use it to make the gorgeous tiramisu on p. 179.

140g dark chocolate
175g self-raising flour
150g caster sugar, plus extra to decorate
125g butter, softened
2 eggs

1 Preheat the oven to 170°C. Grease and line a 1lb loaf tin.
2 Melt the chocolate in a heatproof bowl over a pan of simmering water. Set aside to cool slightly.
3 Put all the remaining ingredients into a large bowl and mix just until smooth, taking care not to overmix.
4 Divide the mixture in half. Fold the melted chocolate into one half.
5 Spoon the two mixtures in alternate drops into the tin, then level the top.
6 Bake for 45–50 minutes, or until risen and just firm to the touch. Leave to rest in the tin for 5 minutes before turning out onto a wire rack to cool.

CHERRY CAKE

SERVES 8–10

We often had Cherry Cake when we were small. My mother always enlisted us to sieve and coat the cherries with flour. It was a big joke if the cherries sank (it was the 1980s and we were easily amused). My father teases that when the cherries sink, it means they're having their annual general meeting at the bottom of the tin. So coat your cherries well, don't bang the oven door and your cake will be studded evenly with ruby red cherries!

140g glacé cherries
100g butter, softened
100g caster sugar
2 eggs
1 tsp vanilla essence

170g plain flour, sieved
60g ground almonds
1 tsp baking powder
2 tbsp milk

1. Preheat the oven to 180°C. Butter and flour a 1lb loaf tin or a 15cm or 20cm round cake tin.
2. Cut the cherries in half and rinse them in a sieve. Dry well with kitchen paper, then dust lightly with a little flour.
3. Cream the butter and sugar together in a bowl until light and fluffy. Add the eggs one by one, mixing well after each addition. Add the vanilla.
4. Fold in the sieved flour, ground almonds and baking powder. Add the prepared cherries and mix carefully. Add the milk, stirring until it's just combined.
5. Spoon the batter into the prepared loaf tin or cake tins. Bake for 45–50 minutes, or until golden and the cake shrinks away from the sides of the tin.

COCONUT LOAF CAKE

SERVES 8–10

Covering cakes with raspberry jam and dipping them in coconut is one of my guilty pleasures. It's quite a dated look but tastes so nice, and that's what it's all about. I like to toast the coconut before I use it as it freshens it up and gives a lovely texture and toasty taste. This is gorgeous with a big pot of tea and it keeps well for a few days.

FOR THE CAKE:
225g butter, softened
225g caster sugar
2 eggs
225g plain flour
1 tsp baking powder
60g desiccated coconut
3 tbsp milk

FOR THE TOPPING:
60g raspberry jam
30g desiccated coconut, toasted

1   Preheat the oven to 180°C. Butter and flour a 1lb loaf tin.
2   Cream the butter and sugar together in a bowl until light and fluffy. Add the eggs one by one, mixing well after each addition.
3   Sieve the flour and baking powder into a bowl, then add to the egg mixture along with the coconut. Beat for a few seconds to combine. Add the milk and mix until just combined.
4   Spoon the batter into the tin and bake for 45–50 minutes, until golden and an inserted skewer comes out clean. Leave in the tin for a minute or so before turning onto a rack to cool.
5   Once the cake is fully cool, spread the jam onto the top and cover in the toasted coconut.

ORANGE BLOSSOM CAKE

SERVES 8–10

This delicately scented cake is lovely with Moroccan mint tea and is a great 4 o'clock cake to have in a tin. It slices well and keeps for a few days in an airtight container. This cake also works well as a base for the trifle on p. 172.

175g butter, softened
175g caster sugar
3 eggs
1 tsp orange blossom water or fresh orange juice
115g plain flour
115g cornflour
1 tsp baking powder
3 tbsp milk

1. Preheat the oven to 180°C. Butter and flour a 1lb loaf tin.
2. Cream the butter and sugar together in a bowl until light and fluffy. Add the eggs one by one, mixing well after each addition. Add the orange blossom water.
3. Sieve the flour, cornflour and baking powder into a bowl, then fold into the egg mixture. Add the milk and mix until the batter has a soft consistency.
4. Spoon the batter into the tin and bake for 35–40 minutes, until an inserted skewer comes out clean. Leave to rest in the tin for 5 minutes before turning out onto a wire rack to cool.

LEMON MADEIRA

SERVES 8–10

....

Lemon Madeira is a classic, the perfect 4 o'clock cake. I usually double this recipe and give one to my parents (whose father doesn't love Lemon Madeira?). You can use any leftover cake for the trifle on p. 172. That's the type of maths I like!

180g self-raising flour
150g caster sugar, plus extra to decorate
125g butter, softened
2 eggs
zest and juice of 1 lemon

1   Preheat the oven to 170°C. Grease and line a 1lb loaf tin.

2   Put all the ingredients into a large bowl and mix just until smooth, taking care not to overmix. Spoon the batter into the tin, level the top and sprinkle with sugar.

3   Bake for about 1 hour, or until risen and just firm to the touch. Leave to rest in the tin for 5 minutes before turning out onto a wire rack to cool and sprinkling more sugar on top.

LAVENDER MADEIRA

SERVES 8–10

The first time I made this gorgeous cake, I was afraid it would taste like potpourri or soap, but it really is lovely! The lavender is subtle and it's probably the nicest-smelling cake you'll ever make. The sugar topping makes it glitter and gives a gorgeous crunch. I like to divide this mixture into smaller loaf tins and give these cakes as presents tied with a purple ribbon and a sprig of lavender.

175g self-raising flour
150g caster sugar, plus extra to decorate
125g butter, softened
2 eggs
1 tbsp lavender flowers, fresh or dried
zest of 1 orange

1   Preheat the oven to 170°C. Grease and line a 1lb loaf tin.
2   Put all the ingredients into a large bowl and mix just until smooth, taking care not to overmix. Spoon the batter into the tin, level the top and sprinkle with sugar.
3   Bake for about 1 hour, or until risen and just firm to the touch. Leave to rest in the tin for 5 minutes before turning out onto a wire rack to cool and sprinkling more sugar on top.

CARAWAY SEED CAKE

SERVES 8–10

This is a traditional cake that older people always seem to remember fondly. I think aniseed is a very particular taste and it makes this an adult cake. It was all the rage in the 19th century, so now you know what to make if you're ever going to a Victorian-themed tea party!

175g self-raising flour
150g caster sugar, plus extra to sprinkle
125g butter, softened
2 eggs
1 tbsp caraway seeds

1   Preheat the oven to 170°C. Grease and line a 1lb loaf tin.
2   Put all the ingredients into a large bowl and mix just until smooth, taking care not to overmix. Pour the batter into the tin and level the top.
3   Bake for about 1 hour, or until risen and just firm to the touch. Leave to rest in the tin for 5 minutes before turning out onto a wire rack to cool.

TEA BRACK

SERVES 8–10

....

I love tea brack. I seem to always be hungry, and tea brack is one of those miraculous 11 o'clock snacks that actually keep me going until lunchtime. My favourite tea to use for this is Pukka Cinnamon and Liquorice as well as Barry's. It really gives the loaf multifaceted shimmering spicy layers! I don't like mixed peel so I used to add orange zest. One day I had no oranges so I used a splash of Cointreau and I've never looked back! This is a beautiful brack with a chewy crust that keeps extremely well.

300ml hot tea (use 2 normal teabags and 1 Earl Grey/cinnamon
  and liquorice/chai, etc.)
180g sultanas
180g raisins
100g dried stoned dates, chopped
1 egg, beaten
225g self-raising flour
150g light brown sugar
1-2 tbsp Cointreau or other orange-flavoured liqueur
2 tsp mixed spice
2 tbsp honey, to glaze

1   The day before you want to make the brack, make the tea and leave to infuse for 15 minutes.
2   Place the sultanas, raisins and chopped dates into a bowl. Remove the teabags from the pot and pour the hot tea over the fruit. Cover and leave overnight to soak.
3   The next day, preheat the oven to 180°C. Line a 1lb loaf tin with parchment paper.
4   Add the beaten egg to the fruit mix along with the flour, sugar, Cointreau and mixed spice. Mix well with a wooden spoon.
5   Spoon the batter into the prepared tin and bake for 1 1/4 to 1 1/2 hours, or until an inserted skewer comes out clean. Leave to rest in the tin for 5 minutes before turning out onto a wire rack to cool. While the cake is still quite warm, brush the top with the honey.

CHAPTER 2

Small Cakes

VANILLA CUPCAKES

MAKES 12 CUPCAKES

Vanilla remains the most popular flavour. It's a great base for different icings too. We always called these Queen Cakes growing up. My favourite cupcake is an uniced vanilla cupcake with 120g sultanas added in. Gorgeous, and perfect with a pot of hot tea. The cupcake took over the world a few years ago although it has since been toppled by the fancy French macaroon. It's still one of my favourite things to bake, as it's so versatile and quick, with great results every time!

220g caster sugar
100g butter, softened
2 eggs
180g plain flour
1½ tsp baking powder
120ml milk
1 tsp vanilla essence
vanilla buttercream, to ice (see p. 194)

1 Preheat the oven to 180°C. Line a 12-hole cupcake tin with paper cases.
2 Cream the sugar and butter together in a bowl until light and fluffy. Add the eggs one by one, mixing well after each addition.
3 Sieve the flour and baking powder together into a bowl, then fold into the egg mixture. Add the milk and vanilla essence and stir until just combined.
4 Use an ice cream scoop or spoon to divide the batter evenly amongst the cake cases. Bake for 15–20 minutes, until the cakes are golden and an inserted skewer comes out clean. Remove the cupcakes from the tin and allow to cool fully on a rack.
5 Once the cakes are fully cooled, you can ice them with vanilla buttercream or an icing of your choice.

BAKEWELL CUPCAKES

MAKES 12 CUPCAKES

My niece Elsie came over one morning to help me bake. Amazingly, she could crack an egg perfectly despite being only three years old! We made lots of different cupcakes, but it was her idea to put jam in one batch. She has a bright baking future!

FOR THE CUPCAKES:
220g caster sugar
100g butter, softened
2 eggs
160g plain flour
100g ground almonds
1 ½ tsp baking powder
150ml milk
1 tsp vanilla essence
6 tbsp raspberry or strawberry jam
12 glace cherries, to decorate

FOR THE ICING:
100g icing sugar, sieved
1 tbsp boiling water

1. Preheat the oven to 180°C. Line a 12-hole cupcake tin with paper cases.
2. Cream the sugar and butter together in a bowl until light and fluffy. Add the eggs one by one, mixing well after each addition.
3. Sieve the flour, ground almonds and baking powder into a bowl, then fold into the egg mixture. Add the milk and vanilla essence and stir until just combined.
4. Use an ice cream scoop or spoon to divide the batter evenly amongst the cake cases, filling each case only halfway. Add 1 teaspoon of jam to each cake case and top with the remaining batter. Bake for 20–25 minutes, until the cakes are golden and an inserted skewer comes out clean. Remove the cakes from the tin and leave to cool fully on a rack.
5. To make the icing, combine the icing sugar with the water and beat until the icing is smooth and is thick enough to coat the back of a spoon. If it's too thin, add more icing sugar or add more water if it's too thick.
6. Once the cupcakes are completely cooled, ice them with the icing and top with a red glace cherry.

PLUM AND CARDAMOM CUPCAKES

MAKES 12 CUPCAKES

These cupcakes are just as lovely uniced. The plums keep the cake moist and are a real fruity surprise when you bite into the cake. No matter how hard and miserable your plums are, baking miraculously brings them to life! Cardamom and plum is a match made in heaven. Beautifully fragrant, a real tea party cake.

FOR THE CUPCAKES:
220g caster sugar
100g butter, softened
2 eggs
4 cardamom pods, crushed and seeds removed
180g plain flour
1 ½ tsp baking powder
120ml milk
1 tsp vanilla essence
6 plums, halved

FOR THE ICING:
55g butter
250g icing sugar, sieved
4 tbsp milk
1 tsp vanilla essence
1 drop of pink food colouring
1 drop of blue food colouring
1 plum, cut into 12 slices,
  to decorate

1 Preheat the oven to 180°C. Line a 12-hole cupcake tin with paper cases.

2 Cream the sugar and butter together in a bowl until light and fluffy. Add the eggs one by one, mixing well after each addition. Add the crushed cardamom seeds.

3 Sieve the flour and baking powder into the bowl. Fold into the mixture, adding the milk and vanilla as you go.

4 Use an ice cream scoop or spoon to divide the batter evenly amongst the paper cases. Top each cake with half a plum. Bake for 20–25 minutes, until golden. Remove the cupcakes from the tin and allow to cool fully on a rack.

5 Meanwhile, to make the icing, beat the butter with half the icing sugar. Add the remaining sugar, milk, vanilla and food colouring and beat well, until the icing is light and fluffy.

6 Spread the icing generously on each cooled cake and top with a slice of plum.

CHOCOLATE AND GINGER CUPCAKES

MAKES 12 CUPCAKES

This is a grown-up cupcake with a warm, spicy hit of ginger and smooth chocolate icing to mellow it all out - it's really something special. Flakes of edible gold leaf would be perfect scattered over the top of these beauties!

100g crystallised stem ginger, plus extra to decorate
120ml milk
220g caster sugar
100g butter, softened
2 eggs
160g plain flour
20g cocoa powder
1 ½ tsp baking powder
chocolate buttercream, to ice (see p. 194)

1   Preheat the oven to 180°C. Line a 12-hole cupcake tin with paper cases.
2   Roughly chop the ginger. Place in a small saucepan with the milk and heat gently for 5–10 minutes. Remove from the heat and leave to cool slightly, then blitz in a food processor.
3   Cream the sugar and butter together in a bowl until light and fluffy. Add the eggs one by one, mixing well after each addition.
4   Sieve the flour, cocoa and baking powder into a bowl, then fold into the egg mixture. Add the gingery milk and stir until just combined.
5   Use an ice cream scoop or spoon to divide the batter evenly amongst the cake cases. Bake for 15–20 minutes, until the cakes are golden and an inserted skewer comes out clean. Remove the cupcakes from the tin and allow to cool fully on a rack.
6   Ice the cooled cakes with chocolate buttercream and decorate with a piece of crystallised stem ginger.

RUM AND RAISIN CUPCAKES

MAKES 12 CUPCAKES

These cupcakes are a real adult treat and are beautiful with a cup of strong coffee. The raisins are soaked in rum overnight, so they are plump and laden with the fragrant alcohol. They are lovely without the icing too and make a comforting dessert with homemade custard poured over.

FOR THE CUPCAKES:
150g sultanas or raisins
100ml dark rum
220g caster sugar
100g butter, softened
2 eggs
160g plain flour
40g ground almonds
1½ tsp baking powder
120ml milk
1 tsp vanilla essence

FOR THE RUM ICING:
55g butter, softened
250g icing sugar, sieved
2 tbsp dark rum
2 tbsp milk

1. Soak the raisins in the rum and leave for a few hours or overnight.

2. Preheat the oven to 180°C. Line a 12-hole cupcake tin with paper cases.

3. Cream the sugar and butter in a bowl until light and fluffy. Add the eggs one by one, mixing well after each addition.

4. Sieve the flour, ground almonds and baking powder into the bowl. Fold into the mixture, adding the milk and vanilla as you go. Finally, drain the raisins and discard any excess rum, then fold them into the batter, setting aside a few for decoration.

5. Use an ice cream scoop or spoon to divide the batter evenly amongst the paper cases. Bake for 20–25 minutes, until golden. Remove the cupcakes from the tin and allow to cool fully on a rack.

6. To make the icing, beat the butter with half the icing sugar. Add the remaining sugar, rum and milk. Beat well, until light and fluffy.

7. Spread the icing generously on each cupcake and top with a few rum-soaked raisins.

ICE CREAM CONE CUPCAKES

MAKES 12 CUPCAKES

The main appeal of these cakes is that they look like ice creams! Kids absolutely love them and can't get over the fact that they are actually cakes. I have tried making these cakes in lots of different ways. You can sit the cones into the cake tin and cook the batter directly in them, but I think it results in a stale cone. Put them together the day you want to eat them. I just used normal vanilla buttercream here, but you could fold some fresh raspberries in to make 'ripple ice cream' or drizzle them with chocolate sauce and toasted nuts.

220g caster sugar
100g butter, softened
2 eggs
180g plain flour
1 ½ tsp baking powder
120ml milk
1 tsp vanilla essence
12 flat-bottomed ice cream cones
vanilla buttercream, to ice (see p. 194)
12 chocolate Flakes, chocolate sprinkles, cherries, etc., to decorate

1 Preheat the oven to 180°C. Line a 12-hole cupcake tin with paper cases.

2 Cream the sugar and butter together in a bowl until light and fluffy. Add the eggs one by one, mixing well after each addition.

3 Sieve the flour and baking powder together in a bowl, then fold into the egg mixture. Add the milk and vanilla essence and stir until just combined.

4 Use an ice cream scoop or spoon to divide the batter evenly amongst the cake cases. Bake for 15–20 minutes, until the cakes are golden and an inserted skewer comes out clean. Remove the cupcakes from the tin and allow to cool fully on a rack.

5 Remove the paper cases and sit the cakes into the ice cream cones. You may need to trim some of the cake off in order to fit the cake in snugly.

6 Make a whipped ice cream shape as you ice the cakes. Stick a Flake into the side or decorate with sprinkles.

MINI BLACK FOREST CAKES

MAKES 12 MINI CAKES

. . . .

A huge multilayered Black Forest Gateau like the one on p. 6 can be difficult to cut into and serve, so I find making small individual cakes is just as easy. You can also omit the liqueur in some to make them child friendly. These freeze very well and can be defrosted and transformed into a beautiful dessert in no time!

115g butter, softened
115g caster sugar
2 eggs
50ml milk
170g self-raising flour
2 tbsp cocoa powder, plus extra to decorate
1 tsp baking powder
115g cherries (frozen, fresh or tinned)
120ml kirsch (cherry liqueur)
150ml cream, whipped
12 fresh cherries, to decorate

1 Preheat the oven to 180°C. Line a 12-hole muffin tin with paper cases.

2 Cream the butter and sugar together in a bowl until light and fluffy. Add the eggs one by one, mixing well after each addition. Mix in the milk.

3 Sieve the flour, cocoa and baking powder together in a bowl, then fold into the egg mix. Stir the cherries through.

4 Divide the batter evenly amongst the muffin cases. Bake for 20–25 minutes, until an inserted skewer comes out clean. Cool on a rack.

5 Once the cakes are fully cooled, peel away the paper cases and divide each cake in three horizontally. Sprinkle each layer with kirsch. Put 1 teaspoon of whipped cream in between each layer and sandwich the layers back together. Dust with cocoa and serve with a cherry on top!

S'MORES CAKES

MAKES 16 CAKES

These are messy, but in a good way! They are an absolutely gorgeous sugar overload that kids and adults will all love. They're best eaten the day they're made, but they usually don't stick around long. When the marshmallow is under the grill you'll need to watch it very carefully, as they are so high in sugar that they tend to catch fire. If you have a little crème brûlée torch it would work perfectly to brown the marshmallow – just make sure you don't flame the paper cases too. Now that is about as 'extreme' as baking gets!

300g digestive biscuits, broken into crumbs
170g butter, melted
40g Demerara sugar
255g dark or milk chocolate chunks
150g marshmallows

1. Preheat the oven to 180°C. Line 2 bun trays with paper cake cases.
2. Stir the biscuit crumbs, melted butter and Demerara sugar together until well combined. Place 2 tablespoons of the crumb mixture into each of the cake cases, then press down firmly with the back of a teaspoon. Bake for 5–10 minutes, until golden.
3. Remove from the oven and top with the chocolate chunks. Return to the oven for another 5 minutes.
4. Turn on the grill. Lightly press some marshmallows into the now-melted chocolate. Grill for 2 minutes, until the marshmallows are puffed up, golden and melting. Allow to cool slightly before eating.

STICKY TOFFEE CAKES

MAKES 8–12 CAKES, DEPENDING ON THE SIZE OF THE TIN

These cakes are absolutely gorgeous! They are perfect for entertaining, as you can prepare them beforehand and then reheat and cover in the addictive toffee sauce. I just use muffin tins and line them with paper cases, since it's a lot easier than greasing and flouring all of the tins. Don't forget to serve with an extra jug of toffee sauce and some freshly whipped cream. The sauce keeps in the fridge for weeks.

FOR THE CAKES:
150g sultanas
120g dates, pitted and chopped
250ml water
1 tsp bread soda
250ml water
60g butter
185g self-raising flour
125g light brown sugar
2 eggs, lightly whisked

FOR THE TOFFEE SAUCE:
140g light brown sugar
90g butter
185ml cream
2 tbsp golden syrup

whipped cream, to serve

1   Preheat the oven to 180°C. Line a muffin tray with 8–12 paper cases (depending on size).

2   Put the sultanas, dates and water into a pan. Bring to the boil, remove from the heat and stir in the bread soda. Add the butter and stir until melted.

3   Sieve the flour into a bowl and stir in the sugar. Make a well in the centre and pour in the date mixture and the eggs. Stir until just combined.

4   Divide the batter evenly amongst the cake cases. Bake for 20 minutes, until an inserted skewer comes out clean.

5   Meanwhile, to make the sauce, put the brown sugar, butter, cream and golden syrup into a medium saucepan over a low heat. Stir for 5 minutes, until the sugar dissolves. Now increase the heat and bring to the boil. Reduce the heat and simmer for 2 minutes. Set aside.

6   To serve, pierce the warm cakes a few times with a skewer, pour over the sauce and serve with cold whipped cream.

RED BERRY AND WHITE CHOCOLATE MUFFINS

MAKES 12 SMALL MUFFINS

···

I always use frozen berries for these muffins, as they hold together when I'm mixing the batter. Somehow I have muffins stored under 'Healthy Foods' in my brain, probably because there's no icing on them! I think they make a great breakfast or 11 a.m. snack and they're perfect for bringing on long car journeys. When I'm driving from Cork to Dublin I often bring muffins and my co-pilot (usually my sister Rosie) is in charge of spotting a garage so we can get tea. This might happen within the first hour of us being on the road. Then for the remaining two hours of the journey we just talk about the muffins and what different flavours we could make – a lot more fun than playing I Spy!

225g plain flour
1 tbsp baking powder
75g caster sugar
1 egg
150ml milk
40ml sunflower oil
1 tsp vanilla essence
160g frozen red berries
70g white chocolate chips

1 Preheat the oven to 190°C. Line a 12-hole muffin tin with paper cases.

2 Sieve the flour and baking powder together in a bowl, then stir in the sugar.

3 Whisk the egg, milk, oil and vanilla together in a jug. Pour into the dry ingredients and mix gently. Fold in the berries and the chocolate chips.

4 Use an ice cream scoop or spoon to divide the batter evenly amongst the muffin cases. Bake for 15–20 minutes, until golden and risen. Remove the muffins from the tin and allow to cool on a rack.

BERRY MUFFINS (GLUTEN FREE)

MAKES 24 MUFFINS

 These muffins are light and airy, full of berries and scented with vanilla. They are best eaten the day they're made but keep for a few days. A good idea for the gluten intolerant in your life is to have these wrapped individually and frozen so they can be brought out for lunches or dessert.

160g potato flour
150g rice flour
1 ½ tsp gluten-free baking powder
1 ½ tsp xanthan gum
½ tsp bread soda
370g caster sugar
1 egg
375ml buttermilk
70g butter, melted
1 tsp vanilla essence
250g mixed berries
vanilla buttercream, to ice (see p. 194)

1 Preheat the oven to 180°C. Line 2 x 12-hole muffin tins with paper cases.
2 Sieve the flours, baking powder, xanthan gum and bread soda into a bowl, then stir through the sugar.
3 Whisk the egg, buttermilk, melted butter and vanilla in a jug. Pour into the flour mixture and briskly combine. Fold in the berries.
4 Use an ice cream scoop or spoon to divide the batter evenly amongst the cake cases. Bake for 15–20 minutes, until golden and puffed up. Remove the muffins from the tin and allow to cool on a rack.
5 Ice with vanilla buttercream once fully cooled or leave uniced.

BLUEBERRY MUFFINS

MAKES 12 MUFFINS

Blueberry muffins are an all-time classic. These little cakes are perfect for school lunchboxes and are also quite happy to sit at home in the cake tin until they're needed with a hot cup of tea!

225g plain flour
1 tbsp baking powder
75g Demerara sugar
1 egg
150ml milk
40ml sunflower oil
1 tsp vanilla essence
160g blueberries

1 Preheat the oven to 190°C. Line a 12-hole cupcake tin with paper cases.

2 Sieve the flour and baking powder together in a bowl, then stir in the sugar.

3 Whisk the egg, milk, oil and vanilla together in a jug. Pour into the dry ingredients and mix gently. Fold in the blueberries.

4 Use an ice cream scoop or spoon to divide the batter evenly amongst the cake cases. Bake for 15–20 minutes, until golden and risen. Remove the muffins from the tin and allow to cool on a rack.

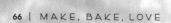

CHOCOLATE PUDDINGS

MAKES 4

....

These puddings always work. As long as you don't leave them in the
oven too long, you will be rewarded with fluffy chocolate sponge and a
hot molten sauce. Amazing with cold whipped cream or fresh
raspberries.

80g caster sugar
160g dark chocolate, chopped
60g milk chocolate, chopped
4 eggs, separated
cream, to serve

1 Preheat the oven to 200°C. Butter 4 ramekins and coat each one with $\frac{1}{2}$ teaspoon sugar.
2 Melt the dark chocolate in a heatproof bowl over a pan of simmering water. Stir and set
   aside once melted and allow to cool.
3 Divide the chopped milk chocolate between the ramekins.
4 Beat the remaining sugar with the egg yolks until pale and creamy. Set aside.
5 In a spotlessly clean, dry bowl, whisk the egg whites until soft peaks form.
6 Fold the melted chocolate into the egg yolk mixture, then carefully fold in the egg whites
   using a metal spoon or spatula.
7 Divide the mixture between the 4 ramekins. Bake for 15–20 minutes, until puffed up. Serve
   immediately with cream.

CUSTARD SLICE

MAKES 8 SLICES

2 sheets ready-made puff pastry, thawed
220g caster sugar
120g custard powder
750ml milk
150ml cream
½ tsp vanilla essence
400g icing sugar, sieved

1 Preheat the oven to 200°C. Line 2 baking trays with parchment paper.
2 Bake the puff pastry sheets on the lined trays for 15–20 minutes, until they are golden and puffed up. Allow the pastry to cool slightly before flattening it with your hand.
3 Combine the sugar and custard powder in a pan, then stir in the milk and cream. Bring to the boil and keep stirring as it thickens. Remove from the heat and leave to cool slightly, then stir in the vanilla.
4 Line a high-edged baking tray with cling film. Place one piece of pastry snugly on the base. Spread the custard thickly over the pastry, then top with the second piece of pastry.
5 Add a few teaspoons of boiling water to the icing sugar until it's thick and spreadable. Spread the icing over the top of the pastry and leave it to set in the fridge. Once set, cut into 8 slices and serve.

CREAM BUNS

MAKES 8 BUNS

....

These cream buns are simply a vehicle for cream and fruit! Loads of fresh berries make the buns really special. They are also lovely with strawberries, drizzled with chocolate or maple syrup and slices of banana.

100g butter
100ml milk
70ml water
140g plain flour, sieved
4 eggs
whipped cream, to serve
fresh berries, to serve
icing sugar, to decorate

1 Preheat the oven to 200°C. Line 2 baking trays with parchment paper.

2 Put the butter, milk and water into a medium saucepan. Heat until the butter melts.

3 Remove the pan from the heat. Beat in the sieved flour really well with a wooden spoon until the mixture becomes smooth and pulls away from the side of the saucepan. Leave to cool for a minute.

4 Beat the eggs in a separate bowl, then gradually add to the dough while beating all the time with the wooden spoon until shiny and glossy.

5 Spoon mounds of the mixture onto the trays, spaced well apart. Bake at 200°C for the first 15 minutes, then lower the temperature to 180°C for the remaining 15 minutes. Make a hole in the side of each bun for the steam to escape and return to the oven for 5 minutes to dry out. Remove from the oven and place on a wire rack to cool completely.

6 Once the buns are fully cooled, cut them in half, fill with whipped cream and berries and dust with icing sugar.

ÉCLAIRS

MAKES 8-10 ÉCLAIRS

I never buy éclairs because they are always covered in a layer of cooking chocolate that cracks the minute you bite into it. I love small éclairs that have a smooth, thick chocolate ganache, freshly whipped cream and a crisp, fresh dough. There's nothing nicer!

FOR THE ÉCLAIRS:
100g butter
100ml milk
70ml water
140g plain flour, sieved
4 eggs

FOR THE CHOCOLATE GANACHE:
100g dark chocolate, chopped
50ml cream

200ml cream, whipped

1 Preheat the oven to 200°C. Line 2 baking trays with parchment paper.

2 Put the butter, milk and water into a medium saucepan. Heat until the butter melts.

3 Remove the pan from the heat and beat in the sieved flour really well with a wooden spoon until the mixture becomes smooth and pulls away from the side of the saucepan. Leave to cool for a minute.

4 Beat the eggs in a separate bowl, then gradually add to the dough while beating all the time with the wooden spoon until shiny and glossy.

5 Leave the mixture to cool before spooning into a piping bag fitted with a 2cm nozzle. Pipe fingers of the mixture onto the trays, spaced well apart.

6 Bake at 200°C for the first 15 minutes, then lower the temperature to 180°C for the remaining 15 minutes. Make a hole in the side of each bun for the steam to escape and return to the oven for 5 minutes to dry out. Remove from the oven and leave to cool completely on a wire rack.

7 To make the ganache, melt the chocolate in a heatproof bowl over a saucepan of simmering water. Stir until smooth. Remove from the heat and leave to cool. Stir in the cream until the sauce is smooth and beginning to thicken.

8 Halve the éclairs and fill with whipped cream, then sandwich together. Using a round-bladed knife, spread the ganache over the tops.

RHUBARB MACAROONS

MAKES 6 MACAROONS

The key to macaroons, supposedly, is to use old egg whites. The day before I make these I usually place the whites in a bowl covered with cling film and leave it to stand on the kitchen counter overnight. I find macaroons amazingly sweet, so I wanted to add a tart filling to balance out all that sugar. Rhubarb is the perfect addition. I roast my rhubarb by chopping it roughly into chunks and covering with about 50ml orange juice, then I slowly roast it in an oven at 160°C for 1 hour. The rhubarb holds its shape but becomes tender and fruitier. Of course, you could stir through some rhubarb conserve if you don't have time to roast some yourself.

200g ground almonds
200g icing sugar
200g caster sugar
50g water
150g egg whites (approx. 4 duck eggs or 6 chicken eggs)

FOR THE FILLING:
60g roasted rhubarb (see note above)
vanilla buttercream icing (see p. 194)

1   Line 2 baking trays with parchment paper.
2   Blitz the almonds and icing sugar in a food processor or sieve together.
3   Place the caster sugar and water in a small saucepan. Stir on a low heat until the sugar dissolves. Increase the heat slightly until the mixture turns syrupy, but it must not caramelise or change colour.
4   While the sugar is heating, divide the egg whites in half. Whisk 75g of the egg whites in a spotlessly clean, dry bowl with an electric mixer until they form stiff peaks. Reduce the speed of the mixer and carefully pour in the hot sugar syrup.
5   Turn the mixer up to high and whip the meringue until it's glossy and white and has cooled. This will take several minutes.
6   Combine the almond mixture and the remaining 75g of egg whites in a large bowl. Spoon the meringue on top of this and fold in carefully with a metal spoon or spatula. Be gentle with the egg whites, as you don't want to knock out the air. Stop mixing once the mixture flows like magma. Don't overmix!

7 Fill a piping bag with a plain tip with the meringue mixture and pipe 4cm rounds of meringue onto the prepared baking trays. Leave to sit for 20 minutes before baking.

8 Preheat the oven to 160°C. Bake each set of macaroons for 15 minutes, turning halfway through the cooking time. The macaroon should lift off the paper easily once it's cooked. Leave to cool for a few minutes on the tray before transferring to a rack.

9 Fold the roasted rhubarb into the buttercream icing. Use this to sandwich the macaroons together at the last minute.

MINI MERINGUES

MAKES 15–20 MINI MERINGUES

6 egg whites
375g icing sugar
60g caster sugar
50ml water
a few drops of food colouring
whipped cream, to serve
fresh fruit, to serve

1 Preheat the oven to 150°C. Line a baking tray with parchment paper or line mini muffin tins with paper cases.

2 Whisk the egg whites and icing sugar in a spotlessly clean, dry bowl with an electric mixer until glossy and it forms stiff peaks.

3 Make a simple coloured syrup by placing the sugar and water into a small pan. Heat gently, stirring to dissolve the sugar. Once the sugar is dissolved, add a few drops of food colouring. Increase the heat and boil until the syrup thickens. It must not caramelise, just let it thicken.

4 Spoon or pipe the stiff meringue mixture into 3cm rounds onto the lined baking tray or into the muffin cases. Using a pastry brush, flick the coloured syrup over the meringues.

5 Bake in the oven for 10–15 minutes, until the meringue lifts off the paper easily. Serve with freshly whipped cream and fruit.

BLUEBERRY POPOVERS

MAKES 2 LARGE POPOVERS

I love having a big breakfast. It's supposed to be the most important meal of the day. On weekdays I just about make it out the door to work with a yoghurt on board and, if I'm organised, porridge. Sundays are my only opportunity for breakfasting like a king - not that I need an excuse! This recipe came about by me lying in bed thinking, 'I love Yorkshire puddings and I love blueberries. Why not?' In America, Yorkshire pudding is known as a popover and there are specialist restaurants dedicated to lots of different flavoured popovers. Dream! You can make this batter the night before and fill it with anything you like - sugared strawberries, raspberries, slices of banana and maple syrup are all amazing additions!

115g plain flour
2 eggs
300ml milk
1 tbsp light brown sugar
10g butter, melted
2 handfuls of frozen blueberries
zest of ½ lemon
1 tbsp caster sugar
sunflower oil
vanilla yoghurt, to serve

1 Sieve the flour into a large mixing bowl. Make a well in the centre and crack in the eggs. Start whisking, gradually bringing in the flour from the sides of the bowl. Add the milk in a steady flow and mix quickly.

2 Dissolve the brown sugar in the melted butter, then whisk into the batter. Leave the batter to stand for 30 minutes or as long as you can. (You could make it the night before.)

3 Preheat the oven to 230°C.

4 Mix together the frozen blueberries, lemon zest and caster sugar. Set aside.

5 Brush some sunflower oil all over 2 x 20cm cake tins. Place the tins in the hot oven until the oil starts to smoke. Quickly fill the tins with the batter.

6 Cook for 5 minutes, then place the blueberry mixture into the centre of each tin. Return to the oven and cook for a further 20–25 minutes, until golden, puffed up and crispy. Ease the popovers out of the tin and onto a plate using a fish slice. Top with a dollop of creamy vanilla yoghurt.

Toffee
Sauce
- x -

Pyramid No. 9

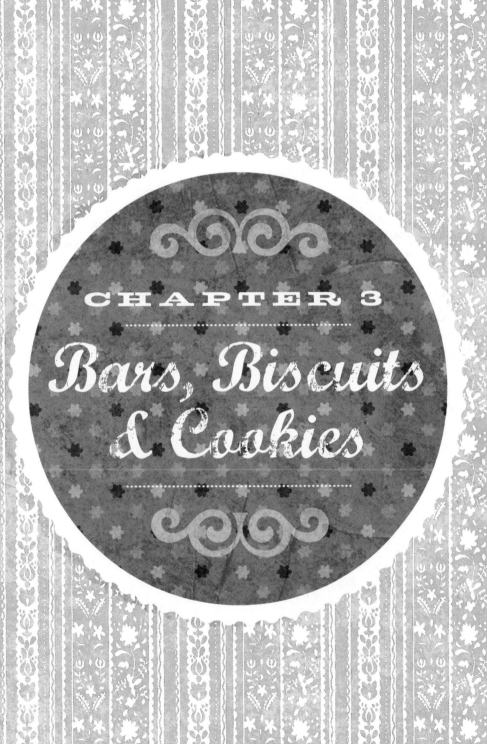

CHAPTER 3

Bars, Biscuits & Cookies

POWER BARS

MAKES 12 BARS

 I love these bars! They're perfect for breakfast, full of magical sunflower seeds and oats that slowly release their energy throughout the morning. If, like me, you find yourself sitting at your desk starving at 11 a.m., then these are great to have in your bag. They keep really well in an airtight tin so they're just the thing to make on Sunday night to keep you going through the week!

150g butter
6 tbsp maple syrup or honey
2 tbsp Demerara sugar
225g oats
150g oatmeal
225g mixed dried fruits and nuts
4 tbsp sunflower seeds

1 Preheat the oven to 200°C. Line a 35cm x 11cm or a 20cm x 23cm tin with parchment paper.

2 Melt the butter, syrup and sugar together in a medium saucepan. Stir in the oats, oatmeal, mixed fruit and nuts. Mix well and press into the tin. Sprinkle the sunflower seeds over the top and press down slightly.

3 Bake for 25 minutes, until golden. Leave to cool slightly, then cut into bars. Store in an airtight tin.

WHITE CHOCOLATE AND RASPBERRY BARS

MAKES 12 BARS

This is one of those recipes that people will ask you for once they taste the bars – or else you'll just be begged to make them again! As well as being the perfect baked treat for 4 o'clock tea, they also make an impressive dessert when dusted with icing sugar and topped with some fresh berries.

200g white chocolate, chopped
75g butter
175g self-raising flour
125g Demerara sugar
3 eggs
250g cream cheese, at room temperature
65g caster sugar
1 egg yolk
1 tsp vanilla essence
350g raspberries (frozen are fine)

1. Preheat the oven to 190°C. Line a 28cm x 20cm tin with parchment paper.
2. Melt the chocolate and the butter in a heatproof bowl set over a pan of simmering water. Set aside to cool slightly.
3. Beat the flour, Demerara sugar and eggs together in a bowl, then add the melted chocolate mix and stir to combine. Pour into the tin and set aside.
4. Beat the cream cheese with the caster sugar, egg yolk and vanilla. Spoon this over the chocolate mix. Marble the two mixes together with the back of a spoon.
5. Bake for 20 minutes, then remove from the oven and scatter the berries over the top, pressing some of them gently into the batter. Bake for a further 25 minutes, until set. Cool in the tin before cutting into 12 bars.

TURTLE BARS

MAKES 12-15 BARS

Turtle bars are a sugary hit of caramel, bitter chocolate and crunchy nuts. They're very easy to make and really tasty. Small kids find these addictive, mostly because of the name, I think!

350g Demerara sugar, divided
350g unsalted butter, softened, divided
220g plain flour
3 tbsp cream
100g pecans
140g dark chocolate chips

1. Preheat oven to 180°C. Line a 23cm x 33cm baking tin with parchment paper.
2. Mix 200g Demerara sugar, 170g butter and the flour in a food processor or rub the butter in with your fingertips until the mixture resembles breadcrumbs. Press the mixture evenly into the prepared tin and bake for about 15 minutes, until golden. Set aside.
3. While the base bakes, place the remaining 180g butter, the remaining 150g Demerara sugar and the cream in a saucepan over a medium heat. Bring to the boil and stir until the sugar dissolves. Leave to boil for 1 minute, until it becomes a thick caramel. Remove from the heat and set aside.
4. Spread the pecans evenly over the biscuit base, then pour over the caramel. Bake for 15 minutes, until the caramel is darker and bubbling. Remove from the oven and immediately sprinkle the chocolate chips over. Allow the chocolate chips to melt slightly.
5. Leave to cool completely before cutting into bars.

OLD HENRY BARS

MAKES 16 BARS

If you mention Old Henry Bars in our house, everyone will think of Henry, our late, great bulldog who loved nothing more than rolling on the driveway when you were trying to reverse your car. There was no point yelling at him because he was mostly deaf, and no point shooing him away because he could only see about one foot in front of him. If you went too close he'd get a fright, because to him it would seem like you came out of nowhere all of a sudden. So all you could do was sit in your car with the engine running and admire poor old Henry as he joyfully rolled around, scratching his back on the autumn leaves.

340g oats
225g light brown sugar
225g butter, melted
4 tbsp smooth peanut butter
150g milk or dark chocolate
a handful of dry-roasted peanuts (optional)

1   Preheat the oven to 180°C. Line a 23cm x 33cm baking tin with parchment paper.

2   Mix the oats, sugar and melted butter together in a bowl. Spread onto the base of the tray and bake for 15 minutes. Remove from the oven, and while still warm, spread the peanut butter over the oat base.

3   Melt the chocolate in a heatproof bowl over a pan of simmering water. Spread the melted chocolate over the peanut butter. Stud with dry-roasted peanuts.

4   Allow to cool slightly, then cut into 16 bars.

JEWELLED RICE BARS

MAKES 10–12 BARS

These are basically a glamorous version of a Rice Krispie square, all dolled up with chocolate and berries and so easy to make. I like to use redcurrants and blackcurrants on top, as they are nice and sharp and balance the sugary marshmallow base.

300g marshmallows
50g butter
1 tbsp golden syrup
250g puffed rice cereal
350g chocolate
200g berries (frozen are fine)

1 Line a 20cm x 28cm tin with parchment paper.
2 Melt the marshmallows and butter in a pan over a low heat, stirring constantly with a silicone spatula. Add the golden syrup, then stir through the puffed rice cereal.
3 Spoon the sticky mixture into the tin. Cover the back of a tablespoon with sunflower oil, then use the spoon to press the mixture down firmly. Set aside.
4 Melt the chocolate in a heatproof bowl over a pan of simmering water. Once melted, pour the chocolate over the base.
5 Leave to cool and set for about 10 minutes before scattering with the berries. Leave to set completely before cutting into squares with an oiled knife.

FIG BARS

MAKES 10 BARS

These bars are perfect if you're on the go. My sister Raedi is a personal trainer and is often going from her yoga class to her running training and so on. She always tries to have snacky things like this in her car. Another of her favourites is the Fig Cake on p. 21. Unfortunately, I have found that just eating these bars alone does not increase my fitness levels, but figs do provide a quick sugar boost before you exercise.

250g dried figs, chopped
120ml boiling water
3 tbsp apple juice
1 tbsp honey
225g plain flour
50g Demerara sugar
2 tbsp cornflour
2 tsp ground ginger
½ tsp baking powder
175g butter

1 Preheat the oven to 180°C. Line a 35cm x 11cm or a 20 cm x 23cm baking tin with parchment paper.
2 Put the figs, boiling water and apple juice into a pan over a medium heat. Simmer for 3–4 minutes, until the figs are soft and have absorbed the liquid. Remove from the heat and leave to cool. Add in the honey and blend using a hand blender or in a food processor until smooth. Set aside.
3 Place the flour, sugar, cornflour, ground ginger and baking powder in a large bowl. Rub in the butter with your fingertips until the mixture resembles breadcrumbs.
4 Press two-thirds of the flour mixture into the lined tin. Press it down well and spread with the fig mixture. Crumble the remaining one-third of the flour mixture over the top. Bake for 30–35 minutes. Allow to cool slightly before cutting into 10 bars.

ROCKY ROAD BROWNIES

MAKES 12-15 BROWNIES

These are like the S'mores Cakes on p. 59 - messy but worth it! Rocky Road has to have both pink and white marshmallows. It's pretty and tastes gorgeous too. The easiest way to cut these is to lightly coat the blade of a sharp knife with sunflower oil so it will cut straight through the marshmallow. Be careful not to overbake the brownie - it should be dense and fudgy.

FOR THE BROWNIES:
200g dark chocolate, chopped
250g icing sugar, sieved
200g butter, softened
3 eggs
110g plain flour

FOR THE TOPPING:
200g dark or milk chocolate, chopped
100g nuts, toasted
100g digestive biscuits, broken up
80g marshmallows

icing sugar, to decorate

1 Preheat the oven to 170°C. Line a 23cm x 33cm baking tin with parchment paper.
2 Melt the chocolate in a heatproof bowl over a pan of simmering water.
3 Beat the icing sugar and butter together in a bowl until light. Add the eggs one at a time, mixing well after each addition. Beat in the flour until just combined. Gradually pour in the melted chocolate and mix well, taking care not to overmix.
4 Pour into the prepared tin and bake for 30 minutes.
5 Meanwhile, mix all the topping ingredients together in a large bowl. Scatter the mixture over the top of the brownies, making sure the chocolate is evenly dispersed. Return the brownies to the oven for 3-5 minutes, until the chocolate has melted slightly and melded the topping ingredients together.
6 Once cool, cut into squares with an oiled knife and dust with icing sugar.

PECAN BROWNIES

MAKES 15-20 BROWNIES

These are the perfect brownies - dense, dark and fudgy with a crisp nutty base. They're amazing with a glass of cold, creamy milk or warmed with a scoop of vanilla ice cream on top.

120g pecans or walnuts, toasted and chopped
250g dark chocolate, chopped
250g butter, cubed
380g Demerara sugar
6 eggs
1 tsp vanilla essence
150g plain flour, sieved

1 Preheat the oven to 180°C. Line a 20cm x 28cm tin with parchment paper.

2 Sprinkle the chopped nuts on the base of the tin.

3 Melt the chocolate and butter in a heatproof bowl over a pan of simmering water. Once melted, stir well and leave to cool slightly.

4 Beat the sugar and eggs with an electric mixer or whisk for 1 minute, until well combined. Stir in the vanilla. Pour in the cooled chocolate and mix well. Fold in the flour until just combined.

5 Pour the batter over the nuts. Bake for 25-30 minutes. Don't overbake, since the brownies will continue to cook for a few minutes after you take them out of the oven. Allow to cool, then cut into 15-20 squares.

HAZELNUT SHORTBREAD

MAKES 2 DOZEN SHORTBREAD BISCUITS

 This shortbread is very simple and quick to make. It's really nice served alongside chocolate mousse as an impressive dessert!

200g butter, softened
110g caster sugar
310g plain flour, sieved
25g ground hazelnuts

1 Cream the butter and sugar together in a bowl until light and fluffy.
2 Add the flour and ground hazelnuts and work into a dough. Flatten into a disc, cover with cling film and chill in the fridge for 10 minutes.
3 Meanwhile, preheat the oven to 180°C. Line 2 baking trays with parchment paper.
4 Roll out the chilled dough on a lightly floured surface until it's 3mm thick. Cut into shapes using a biscuit cutter and place on the prepared trays.
5 Bake for 10–12 minutes, depending on size, until pale golden. Leave to cool on the trays for a minute before transferring to a rack.

Leabharlanna Poibli Chathair Bhaile Átha Cliath
Dublin City Public Libraries

JAMMY DODGERS

MAKES 24 BISCUITS

These biscuits are so cute! I initially made them because I wanted to see how lovely they would look, but it turns out they taste gorgeous too. Perfect for Valentine's Day and a great way to showcase all of your favourite jams - blackberry, apricot and strawberry all work well. These keep in a tin for 3 days with the jam or 1 week without the jam.

300g plain flour
175g butter
50g caster sugar, plus extra to decorate
½ tsp vanilla essence
a few tablespoons of raspberry jam

1 Preheat the oven to 180°C. Line a baking tray with parchment paper.
2 Put the flour, butter, sugar and vanilla into a food processor and blend until a dough forms and it all clumps together. Flatten the dough onto a plate and place in the fridge for 10 minutes.
3 Roll the dough out until it's 3mm thick, then cut into rounds. Cut smaller heart shapes out of half of the rounds. (You can use the scraps of dough to make more or just cook the small hearts for 6–8 minutes.)
4 Bake for 8–10 minutes, until slightly golden. Cool on a rack.
5 Sandwich the biscuits together with the jam, with a round biscuit on the bottom and a biscuit with a heart cut-out on top. Sprinkle with sugar.

LEMON DROPS

MAKES 20–25 BISCUITS

These biscuits are perfect with tea after dinner. They are light and have a fresh citrus sweetness. Orange or lime zest also works perfectly. These biscuits are great to make if you have kids to help, as they can roll the dough into balls and flatten them with a teaspoon. A mundane task for an adult, but riveting if you're a four-year-old!

200g butter, softened
50g icing sugar, sieved, plus extra to decorate
zest of 1 lemon
200g plain flour
¼ tsp baking powder

1 Preheat the oven to 180°C. Lightly grease 2 baking trays.
2 Cream the butter and icing sugar together in a bowl until light and fluffy. Add the lemon zest. Quickly beat in the flour and baking powder until just combined.
3 Roll teaspoons of the mixture into balls. Place on the baking tray and flatten slightly with a teaspoon, making a 'thumbprint'.
4 Bake for 10–15 minutes, until lightly golden. Cool on a rack and dust with icing sugar.

CHOCOLATE CHIP NUT COOKIES

MAKES 24 COOKIES

These cookies are a traditional favourite and in my opinion have to be made with hazelnuts. They're beautiful with a glass of cold milk or milky coffee. It's really handy to have a log of this cookie dough in the freezer - you can cut it straight from frozen and they bake in minutes.

The hazelnuts can be toasted by placing them on a flat baking tray and roasting in a preheated oven at 180°C for 5-10 minutes. Keep an eye on them so they don't burn. Once toasted, place the nuts in a clean tea towel and rub off the skins. Discard the skins and chop the nuts.

These cookies keep in an airtight tin for at least 2 weeks. It's a great recipe to have!

175g butter, softened
100g caster sugar
1 tsp vanilla essence
175g plain flour
85g wholemeal flour
60g hazelnuts, toasted and chopped
60g chocolate chips

1 Beat the butter, sugar and vanilla in a medium bowl for about 1 minute, until smooth.
2 Sieve the two flours in a bowl, then add to the butter and sugar mixture. Beat until just combined. Add the nuts and chocolate chips. Beat again until the nuts and chocolate are evenly dispersed.
3 Form the dough into a log and wrap in cling film. Place in the fridge for a few hours or overnight. It also freezes very well at this stage.
4 Preheat the oven to 180°C. Line 2 baking trays with parchment paper.
5 Using a sharp knife, cut the dough log into 24 slices. Space each slice about 3cm apart on the trays. Bake for 10-15 minutes, or until golden. Leave to cool slightly on the tray, then transfer to a rack.

PEANUT BUTTER AND SESAME COOKIES

MAKES 36 REGULAR OR 60 BITE-SIZED COOKIES

I'm always looking for The Perfect Peanut Butter Cookie. It's a great cookie recipe to have, but this one has an ace up its sleeve. By rolling the dough in sesame seeds it gives a gorgeous nutty texture without compromising the buttery smoothness of the cookie itself. These cookies keep for about a week in a sealed tin and can be made into tiny bite-size cookies to have with coffee too. You could also drizzle melted chocolate over them to make them even nicer!

125g butter, softened
85g caster sugar
80g Demerara sugar
125g smooth peanut butter
¼ tsp vanilla essence
200g plain flour
1 tsp bread soda
50g sesame seeds

1 Preheat the oven to 170°C. Line 2 baking trays with parchment paper.

2 Cream the butter and both sugars together in a bowl until soft and fluffy. Add the peanut butter and vanilla and mix well.

3 Sieve the flour and bread soda together in a bowl, then add to the peanut butter mixture. Combine well but don't overbeat.

4 Roll teaspoons of the dough into balls. Roll the balls in the sesame seeds and place on the lined baking tray. Flatten slightly.

5 Bake for 10 minutes (or 7 minutes for tiny cookies), until golden brown. Leave to cool slightly on the tray, then transfer to a rack.

CANADIAN ROCKY JUMBLES

MAKES 24 COOKIES

These are a substantial cookie, full of oats and nuts. I like to keep one log of dough in the freezer to use at a later date. It always comes in handy!

225g butter, softened
225g caster sugar
200g Demerara sugar
2 eggs, beaten
1 tbsp maple syrup
180g plain flour
1 tsp bread soda
250g oats
80g pecans, chopped
50g icing sugar
extra pecans for the top of each biscuit

1 Cream the butter and the sugars together in a large bowl until light and fluffy. Add the eggs and maple syrup. Beat well, until blended.

2 Sieve the flour and bread soda into the egg mixture. Mix until just combined. Fold in the oats and chopped pecans. Divide the dough in half and roll each half into a log.

3 Dust the countertop with icing sugar and roll the dough log in it until it's completely covered in sugar. Wrap the dough in parchment paper and chill in the fridge for 30 minutes, or until firm.

4 Preheat the oven to 180°C. Line 2 baking trays with parchment paper.

5 Remove the dough from the fridge, cut into 1cm-thick slices and spread out evenly on the prepared baking trays. Press a pecan half firmly into the centre of each biscuit. Bake for 10–12 minutes, until light brown and crisp. Leave to cool on the trays for a minute before transferring to a rack.

CHAPTER 4

Pies &
Tarts

SHORTCRUST PASTRY

MAKES ENOUGH FOR 1 TART OR PIE (BASE AND TOP)

I really am not the best at pastry and have tried so many different recipes. I'm better at kneading. My saving grace has been the food processor! It's so easy - you can just tip everything in, hit a button and a whole world of buttery, crisp, perfect pastry will be yours. You will no longer be afraid of making apple tarts, cherry pies or lemon tarts. If you're not a strong country girl like me, then you probably will be able to make light and lovely pastry by hand!

240g plain flour
150g cold butter, diced
30g icing sugar
1 egg, beaten

1   Put the flour, butter and sugar into a bowl. Rub in the butter with your fingertips until it resembles breadcrumbs. (Alternatively, you can also do this in a food processor.)

2   Add the egg and gently work in with a round-bladed knife or in the food processor to bind the ingredients together. Don't knead.

3   Flatten the pastry into a disc and cover with cling film. Leave to rest in the fridge for 30 minutes before using. (Or the pastry can be frozen at this stage, double wrapped in cling film, for up to 3 months.)

4   To bake a pastry shell blind, simply divide the pastry disc in half. On a lightly floured surface, roll out the pastry into a flat disc a little larger than the diameter of your tin. Carefully roll the pastry onto your rolling pin and unfurl it over the tin. Gently press the pastry into the corners and smooth using a small ball of pastry. Trim the excess pastry from the top edges. Place a large circle of parchment paper over the pastry and snugly press it so that it covers all of the pastry and comes up over the sides. Fill with baking beans or dried pulses. Bake in a preheated oven at 180°C for 15-20 minutes, until the pastry is golden. Remove the parchment and baking beans and return to the oven for a further 5 minutes.

APPLE GALETTE

SERVES 8

This tart is so pretty and versatile. You can use any type of fruit or berries. Blueberries, plums, apples, blackberries and rhubarb all work really well. If pastry isn't your thing, then this tart is a great place to start, as the pastry is almost dough-like and is very forgiving. Part of its charm is its rustic look!

FOR THE PASTRY:
200g plain flour
140g cold butter, cubed
25g caster sugar
1 egg, beaten

FOR THE FILLING:
70g almonds
1 tbsp plain flour
70g butter
60g caster sugar
1 egg
3 eating apples (such as Pink Lady, Cox Pippin or Golden Delicious)
1 tbsp milk
1 tbsp light brown sugar

custard or cream, to serve

1 Preheat the oven to 190°C. Grease a large baking sheet.
2 Sieve the flour into a bowl. Rub in the butter with your fingertips until the mixture resembles breadcrumbs. Stir in the sugar and mix in the egg.
3 Knead quickly and shape into a disc. Cover with cling film and place in the fridge for 10 minutes.
4 Meanwhile, make the filling. Put the almonds and flour into a food processor and blitz. Add the butter and caster sugar and blitz again. Add the egg and blitz until it's a smooth paste.
5 On a lightly floured surface, roll out the pastry to form a 30cm circle. Place onto the greased baking sheet. Spread the almond mixture over the pastry, leaving a 5cm border around the edges.
6 Thinly slice the apples (you can peel them for a nicer texture or leave them unpeeled if you want to see the red or green skin). Layer them on top of the almond mixture in a nice pattern, then fold up the sides of the pastry to keep the almond mix and apples safely inside. Brush the edges with milk and sprinkle with brown sugar. Bake for 25–30 minutes, until golden. Allow to cool on a rack or serve warm with custard or cream.

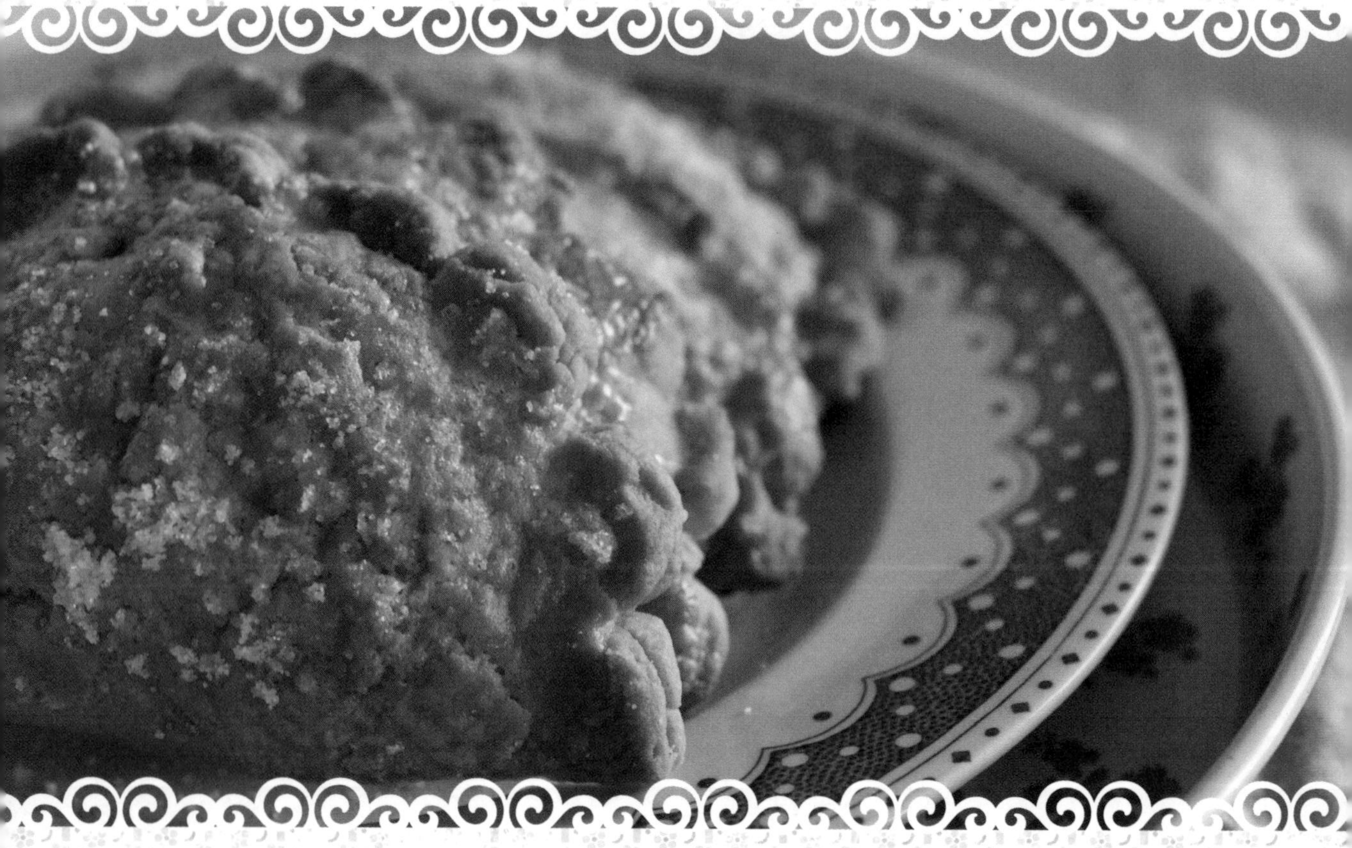

APPLE HAND PIES

MAKES 8 PIES

These are just the cutest apple tarts ever – an individual pie for
everyone. They're sweet Cornish pasties and you don't even need to go
down the mines to merit one! You can use any filling for these beauties.
Sultanas work well in the apple ones, or try rhubarb and strawberry,
blackberry and apple or peach and raspberry. As with Cornish pasties,
these travel well in lunchboxes once they're wrapped up.

4 Bramley apples
2 eating apples (such as Cox Pippin or Golden Delicious)
zest of 1 lemon
1 tbsp light brown sugar
2 tbsp water
1 tsp butter
½ tsp mixed spice
1 batch shortcrust pastry (see p. 115)
1 egg, beaten
caster sugar, to decorate

1   Preheat the oven to 180°C. Line 2 baking trays with parchment paper.
2   Peel and chop all of the apples into cubes. Place in a medium saucepan with the lemon zest,
    sugar, water, butter and mixed spice. Cook gently, stirring with a wooden spoon, for 10
    minutes, until the apples are fairly broken down. Leave to cool.
3   Roll out the pastry on a lightly floured surface. Use a saucer or similar-sized cutter to trace
    out the circle shape of the pies.
4   Fill half of each circle with 2 or 3 teaspoons of apple, leaving a border around the edge. Fold
    over the pastry to make a semi-circle, then pinch the edges together or press with a fork.
    Brush with the beaten egg and sprinkle caster sugar over each pie.
5   Bake for 25-30 minutes, until golden. Leave to cool on a wire rack or serve warm.

MILK TART

SERVES 10–12

Milk Tart is a traditional South African dessert that we used to always have at barbeques and get-togethers in Zimbabwe when we were small. Someone always brought shortbread and there was always Milk Tart. The traditional tart is a vanilla-scented set custard lightly dusted with cinnamon. It really is beautiful. I made a marbled chocolate version of this on the blog and couldn't wait to taste it, as I'd been planning for so long to make a chocolate version. I made a cocoa-based pastry and mixed one-third of the filling with dark melted chocolate. All I can say is, don't mess with a classic! I've stuck with vanilla and cinnamon ever since. I use the usual shortcrust pastry for this and I add 1 tsp cinnamon to it. Try to make your pastry very thin, as this tart is all about lightness and a crisp, buttery pastry with the smooth vanilla filling.

1 litre milk
1 tbsp butter
2 eggs
150g caster sugar
3 tbsp cornflour
3 tbsp plain flour
1 tbsp vanilla essence
1 blind-baked pastry case (add 1 tsp cinnamon to the pastry dough from p. 115)
ground cinnamon, to decorate

1 Bring the milk and butter to the boil in a medium saucepan. Really keep an eye on it, as the milk will boil over the second you look away!

2 Cream the eggs, sugar, cornflour, flour and vanilla essence together in a bowl. Add some of the hot milk to the egg mixture, then pour it all back into the pan. Heat for 5–10 minutes, until the mixture thickens. Keep stirring and don't allow the mixture to boil.

3 Pour into the pastry case. Leave to cool (but not in the fridge, as it will make the pastry damp) and sprinkle generously with cinnamon before serving.

RICOTTA TART

SERVES 8–10

Ricotta has an unusual grainy texture and this zesty tart is really lovely served with fresh berries or fruit. Pine nuts are traditionally sprinkled all over the top of a ricotta tart and they're especially gorgeous if you toast them. Always keep your pine nuts in the freezer, as they spoil if kept in the cupboard for too long.

450g ricotta
80g caster sugar
3 eggs
zest of 1 lemon
4 tbsp lemon juice
1 blind-baked pastry case in a 28cm loose-bottomed tin (see p. 115)
a handful of toasted pine nuts, to decorate
icing sugar, to decorate

1. Preheat the oven to 180°C.
2. Put the ricotta, sugar, eggs and lemon zest and juice into a food processor or large bowl and mix until well combined. Pour into the cooled pastry case.
3. Bake in the middle of the oven for 20 minutes, until set. Allow to cool, then remove from the tin.
4. Sprinkle with pine nuts and dust generously with icing sugar.

STRAWBERRY AND RHUBARB TART

SERVES 6-8

....

Whenever I'm baking or cooking, I always think about who I'm cooking for or why I'm doing it - the chocolate cake for my sister's birthday, the biscuits to bring into work to make Monday easier, the pastel-coloured cupcakes for a friend's baby shower. I think it's because when we were small there was a hierarchy in the kitchen. The eldest would be in charge of making the garlic bread, second in command would assemble the salad and so on. The lowest job on the list was setting the kitchen table. I used to hate getting stuck with this, until one day my mother said to think about who I was doing it for and make it the best table setting I'd ever done. I pulled daffodils from the garden and stuck them in a jam jar, wrote out name tags for each setting and made sure the napkins were all folded perfectly.

Last year, my much-loved granny was in the brilliant Marymount Hospice in Cork. All of the family gathered from around the globe to say our goodbyes. The day she passed away, everyone came to my parents' house for tea afterwards. It's a weird limbo situation when you just have to sit around chatting for hours and drinking tea while visitors come and go to pay their respects. And that was the day that I made the most amazing Strawberry and Rhubarb Tart. The pastry was buttery and crisp, lighter than I'd ever made. The rhubarb and strawberries had come together beautifully. The kitchen smelled reassuringly fragrant and buttery. I had made it to comfort my family and every crumb of it was put to good use. Those are the days when baking really is something powerful.

400g rhubarb, chopped
400g strawberries, hulled and sliced thickly
1 tsp vanilla essence
50g caster sugar, plus extra to decorate
1 tbsp cornflour
1 batch shortcrust pastry (see p. 115)
1 egg, beaten
freshly whipped cream, to serve

1 Preheat the oven to 180°C.

2 Place the chopped rhubarb, strawberries and vanilla into a bowl. Stir to combine. Sprinkle over the sugar, then sieve over the cornflour. Stir to coat all of the fruit.

3 Roll out two-thirds of the pastry to cover the base of a 28cm loose-bottomed tart tin. Spread the fruit evenly over the base. Roll out the remaining pastry and cover the fruit.

4 Pinch the pastry edges together to seal. Cut a few slits in the top of the tart to let the juices escape. Brush with the beaten egg and sprinkle with sugar.

5 Bake for 35–40 minutes, until the pastry is golden and the bright pink juices begin to bubble up through the top. Allow to cool or serve warm with lots of freshly whipped cream.

RASPBERRY MACAROON TART

SERVES 8-10

This is a lovely light tropical tart. The lime zest in the coconut topping is fresh and summery. It's so easy to make and is a great recipe for kids to help with. You can leave out the lime zest and jam if you like and drizzle the top with melted chocolate instead.

FOR THE BASE:
75g caster sugar
50g butter, softened
1 egg yolk
90g plain flour
¼ tsp baking powder
200g raspberry jam

FOR THE TOPPING:
2 eggs
60g caster sugar
zest of 1 lime
160g desiccated coconut
20g flaked almonds

1. Preheat the oven to 180°C. Butter and flour a 28cm loose-bottomed tart tin.
2. Cream the sugar, butter and egg yolk together in a bowl until light and fluffy. Sieve the flour and baking powder into the bowl and stir in until the mixture clumps together and resembles breadcrumbs. Press into the base of the tin with floured fingers. Spread the base with the jam.
3. To make the topping, lightly beat the eggs and sugar together to combine. Fold in the lime zest and coconut. Spread the topping over the jam. Sprinkle with the almond flakes and press down gently.
4. Bake for 30 minutes, or until slightly browning and golden. Cool in the tin for a few minutes before turning out onto a serving plate.

CITRUS TART

SERVES 8-10

Everyone loves lemon tarts, but this recipe uses lime too for a fresh, zingy and light taste. It's a gorgeous, simple tart that you will make over and over. Serve with lots of freshly whipped cream or fresh raspberries.

½ batch shortcrust pastry (see p. 115)
4 eggs
180g caster sugar
finely grated zest of 1 lemon
finely grated zest of 1 lime
100ml cream
50ml lemon juice (or the juice of 1 lemon)
50ml lime juice (or the juice of 2 limes)
freshly whipped cream, to serve
fresh raspberries, to serve

1. Preheat the oven to 180°C. Roll the pastry out to line a loose-bottomed 24cm tart tin or 6 individual tins.

2. Line the tin or tins with parchment paper and fill with baking beans. Bake for 10 minutes. Remove the beans and paper and cook for another 10 minutes. Remove from the oven and set aside.

3. Whisk the eggs and sugar together in a bowl. Stir in the zest, cream and lemon and lime juice. Transfer to a jug.

4. Put the tart onto a baking tray, then place in the oven. Slowly and carefully pour the filling into the pastry case. Bake for 35-40 minutes for 1 large tart or 15-20 for individual tarts. Remove from the oven when there is still a slight wobble in the middle and the filling is nearly set. It will continue to set as it cools on a wire rack. Serve with cold whipped cream and raspberries.

FRUIT TART

SERVES 8-10

 This is the perfect tart to show off fresh berries and fruit. Simply bake the pastry case blind, fill with custard cream and arrange your berries as beautifully as you can. It's a real pastry shop tart that is lovely for a special summer occasion. This is best eaten on the day it's made.

½ batch shortcrust pastry (see p. 115)
1 egg, separated
50g caster sugar
30g custard powder
225ml milk
1 tsp vanilla essence
250ml cream, softly whipped
a selection of berries, such as strawberries, blackberries, raspberries
  and/or redcurrants
1 tbsp redcurrant jelly
1 tbsp boiling water

1 Preheat the oven to 180°C.

2 Roll out the pastry to fit a 28cm loose-bottomed tart tin. Line the tin with the pastry. Cover the pastry with parchment paper and baking beans. Bake for 20-25 minutes, until golden and fully cooked. Remove the paper and beans. Brush the base and insides with egg white and return to the oven for a further 5 minutes to seal. Set aside.

3 Meanwhile, combine the sugar and custard powder in a pan. Stir in the milk. Bring to the boil and keep stirring as it thickens. Remove from the heat and leave to cool slightly, then stir in the egg yolk and vanilla. Cover the top of the custard with cling film or a butter wrapper so it doesn't form a skin.

4 Once the pastry case has fully cooled, remove it from the tin and place on a serving plate.

5 Fold the whipped cream into the cooled custard. Fill the pastry case with the pastry cream and smooth the surface evenly. Arrange the berries neatly on top.

6 Mix the jelly with the boiling water in a bowl, then sieve. Gently brush the fruits with the redcurrant jelly glaze.

JAM LATTICE TARTLETS

MAKES 6–12 TARTLETS, DEPENDING ON THE SIZE OF YOUR TINS

These little tarts are so cute and are a great way to use some of your favourite jams. Black cherry conserve, strawberry and vanilla, apricot and gooseberry all work really well. You can make these tarts in any size or shape. I love the look of hearts – so traditional, like something from *Alice in Wonderland*! I love using individual heart-shaped tins, but shallow cupcake tins also work well.

1 batch shortcrust pastry (see p. 115)
half a jar of your favourite jam
1 egg, beaten
caster sugar, to sprinkle over
cream, to serve

1   Preheat the oven to 180°C.
2   Roll out the chilled pastry and use a pastry cutter or knife to shape the pastry for the tins you are using. Use two-thirds of the pastry for the cases. Keep the remaining one-third for the top.
3   Place the pastry in the tin(s). Cover each tart with a paper muffin case and fill with baking beans or lentils.
4   Bake for 5–10 minutes, until slightly golden. Remove the paper case and baking beans. Add a tablespoon or so of jam into each case, until full.
5   Roll out the remaining one-third of the pastry and cut into strips. Use the beaten egg to 'glue' the strips in place with the pastry case to form a lattice effect. Glaze with more of the beaten egg and sprinkle with sugar.
6   Bake for 10–15 minutes (this depends on how big the tartlets are), until the pastry is golden and the jam is bubbling. Leave to cool in the tin for a few minutes before removing.

CHOCOLATE TARTLETS

MAKES 8-10 TARTLETS

These little tartlets are like mini Pop Tarts and are gorgeous with coffee. They're a great way to use up leftover pastry and can be covered and kept in the fridge overnight before baking for breakfast.

100g dark, milk or white chocolate, chopped
50g ground almonds or hazelnuts
2 tbsp cream
½ batch shortcrust pastry (see p. 115)
milk, for brushing

OPTIONAL EXTRAS:
1 tbsp Frangelico or other liqueur
zest of 1 orange
½ tsp mixed spice
a pinch of chilli powder

1. Preheat the oven to 180°C. Line 2 baking trays with parchment paper.
2. Melt the chocolate in a heatproof bowl over a pan of simmering water. Once melted, stir the chocolate until smooth. Add the ground nuts and leave to cool slightly. Stir in the cream, then add any optional extras. The mixture will be thick and grainy.
3. Roll out the pastry on a lightly floured surface. Cut into 16-20 uniform rectangles.
4. Spread 1 teaspoon or so of the chocolate mixture into the centre of half of the pastry rectangles. Leave a border around the edges. Sandwich the second piece of pastry on top of the chocolate. Brush lightly with milk and pinch the edges together to seal or crimp with a fork.
5. Place the tartlets onto the trays. Bake for 15-20 minutes, until golden. Transfer to a wire rack to cool.

BRAINSE DOMHNACH MIDE
DONAGHMEDE LIBRARY
TEL. 8482833

CHOCOLATE WONTONS

MAKES 12 WONTONS

These little pastry parcels are a lovely way to finish a meal with coffee. Served warm, your guests will be very impressed! Make them even more special by sprinkling with flakes of sea salt. The perfect solution when you have leftover filo pastry.

100g butter, melted
250g dark chocolate, chopped
2 tbsp cream
1 packet of filo pastry, defrosted
sea salt, to sprinkle over

1. Preheat the oven to 180°C. Brush the holes of a 12-hole muffin tin with some of the melted butter.

2. Melt the chocolate in a heatproof bowl set over a pan of simmering water. Stir until smooth, then remove from the heat. Once the chocolate has cooled slightly, beat in the cream. Set aside.

3. Cut the pastry sheets in half. Lay one sheet into a buttered muffin hole and brush with butter. Lay another sheet over and brush with butter again.

4. Place 2 tablespoons of chocolate in the centre of the pastry. Gather up the corners and fold over neatly, sealing with melted butter as you go. Repeat for all 12 wontons, then sprinkle the tops sparingly with sea salt.

5. Bake for 10–15 minutes, until the pastry is golden. Leave in the tins for a few minutes before transferring to a wire rack to cool.

CHAPTER 5

Breads

WHITE YEAST BREAD

MAKES 1 LOAF

Yeast bread is so rewarding to make. The kneading is calming and you really feel brilliant to be making one of the most basic staple foods. Of course, if you have a mixer, then by all means use the dough hook, it halves the time! I always put my yeast dough in the hot press to rise. It's the perfect safe place, with indirect, mild warmth. I often keep plastic disposable shower caps from hotels to use for covering my dough! I know, it's a total dough brainer.

500g strong white flour
1 x 7g sachet fast-action yeast
2 tsp salt
1 tsp caster sugar
300ml warm water
1 tbsp vegetable oil, plus extra for greasing

1   Mix together the flour, yeast, salt and sugar in a large bowl. Add the warm water and vegetable oil. Mix quickly with a wooden spoon until you have a soft, pliable dough.

2   Turn the dough out of the bowl onto a lightly floured surface and knead for 10 minutes, until the dough is smooth and elastic.

3   Shape the dough and tuck into an oiled and floured 2lb loaf tin. Cover with a clean tea towel and leave to rise in a warm, draught-free place for 45 minutes, or until doubled in size

4   Preheat the oven to 220°C. Once the bread is risen, dust the top of the loaf lightly with flour. Bake for 30–35 minutes, until the crust is golden and the bread comes out of the tin easily.

5   Remove from the tin and return to the oven for 5 minutes. The base should sound hollow when tapped. Leave to cool on a rack.

SODA BREAD

MAKES 1 LOAF

A good soda bread is hard to beat: white soda bread spread with jam, brown soda bread with marmalade, sultana soda bread with butter, and chocolate spread on chocolate chip soda! This is quick and easy to make. This basic dough can be transformed by adding 100g sultanas or chocolate chips or using half wholemeal flour.

450g plain flour
1 tsp bread soda
1 tsp salt
350ml buttermilk

1. Preheat the oven to 220°C. Dust a heavy baking tray with flour.
2. Sieve the flour, bread soda and salt into a large bowl. Make a well in the centre and add the buttermilk. Use your hands or a round-bladed knife to bring the dough together until it's craggy and soft.
3. Wash your hands, then transfer the dough to a floured surface and shape into a round loaf, patting gently as you turn it. Gently lift the loaf onto the baking tray. Using a sharp knife, score a cross shape onto the top of the loaf.
4. Bake immediately for 20 minutes, then lower the oven to 200°C and bake for a further 20 minutes, until golden and risen and the base sounds hollow when tapped.

SEED SODA BREAD (GLUTEN FREE)

MAKES 1 LOAF

I always think that bread is one of the main things a coeliac misses out on. Most gluten-free breads you buy are vacuum packed and made to last for months – not the most appetising! This bread is quick and easy to make, the perfect gift for the gluten-free people in your life.

280g rice flour
100g potato flour
1 tsp bread soda
1 tsp xanthan gum
1 tsp gluten-free baking powder
1 tsp salt
1 tbsp linseeds
1 tbsp sesame seeds
1 tbsp sunflower seeds
1 egg, beaten
300-350ml buttermilk

1   Preheat the oven to 200°C. Dust a heavy baking tray with flour.
2   Sieve the flours, bread soda, xanthan gum, baking powder and salt together into a large bowl. Stir in the seeds.
3   Whisk the egg and buttermilk together in a jug.
4   Make a well in the centre of the flour, then pour in the milk mixture. Combine gently and quickly using your hands or a round-bladed knife.
5   Turn out onto a lightly floured surface. Shape the dough into a circular loaf and place on the baking tray or into an oiled and floured 2lb loaf tin. Cut a cross or line down the middle.
6   Bake for 10 minutes, then reduce the temperature to 180°C and bake for a further 20 minutes. When the bread is done, the base should sound hollow when tapped.

PLAIN SCONES

MAKES 12 SCONES

Scones are one of my favourite comfort foods. They're so quick and easy to make and the ingredients are always in the house. When we were teenagers, my mother used to bake trays and trays of scones on a Sunday morning and we could all sit around eating them with lots of butter and countless cups of tea recounting Saturday night's happenings. I think that's the beauty of scones – they make you sit down and chat!

500g plain flour
2 tsp baking powder
2 tbsp caster sugar, plus extra to sprinkle on top
110g butter, cubed
300ml milk
1 egg, beaten

1. Preheat the oven to 200°C. Dust a heavy baking tray with flour.
2. Sieve the flour and baking powder into a large bowl, then stir in the sugar. Rub in the butter with your fingertips until the mixture resembles breadcrumbs.
3. Make a well in the middle of the bowl. Pour in the milk and mix with your hands to form a soft dough.
4. Wash your hands and tip the scone dough onto a lightly floured surface. Flatten the dough until it's about 3cm high. Use a scone cutter or knife to divide the dough into 12 scones.
5. Gently place the scones onto the floured tray and brush with the beaten egg. Sprinkle sugar over the top. Bake for 15–20 minutes, until risen and lightly golden. Allow the scones to cool on a wire rack.

CINNAMON RAISIN SCONES

MAKES 12 SCONES

I only make these scones in winter or when the weather is cold and you need some warmth and spice! The house always smells amazing and they make a great breakfast treat too. These are really lovely spread with raspberry jam.

500g plain flour
2 tsp baking powder
½ tsp mixed spice
5 tbsp caster sugar, divided
110g butter, cubed
160g sultanas
300ml milk
1 egg, beaten
½ tsp cinnamon

1. Preheat the oven to 200°C. Dust a heavy baking tray with flour.
2. Sieve the flour, baking powder and mixed spice into a large bowl, then stir in 2 tablespoons sugar. Rub in the butter with your fingertips until the mixture resembles breadcrumbs. Stir in the sultanas.
3. Make a well in the middle of the bowl. Pour in the milk and mix with your hands to form a soft dough.
4. Wash your hands and tip the scone dough onto a lightly floured surface. Flatten the dough until it's about 3cm high. Use a scone cutter or knife to divide the dough into 12 scones.
5. Gently place the scones onto the floured tray and brush with the beaten egg. Mix the remaining 3 tablespoons sugar with the cinnamon, then sprinkle the cinnamon sugar over the top. Bake for 15–20 minutes, until risen and lightly golden. Allow the scones to cool on a wire rack.

FESTIVE SCONE WREATH

SERVES 10

This wreath makes a really lovely addition to a Christmas hamper or just as a gift wrapped with cellophane and tied with a red ribbon. I love to break off the scones and toast them, then spread with lots of lovely brandy or rum butter, a real seasonal treat!

340g plain flour
1 tsp baking powder
½ tsp mixed spice
1 tbsp Demerara sugar
80g butter, cubed
1 egg
160ml milk
225g mincemeat
1 egg beaten with 1 tbsp milk, to glaze
50g flaked almonds
icing sugar, to decorate

1. Preheat the oven to 180°C. Butter and flour a round ring mould cake tin.
2. Sieve the flour, baking powder and mixed spice into a large bowl, then stir through the sugar. Rub in the butter with your fingertips until the mixture resembles breadcrumbs.
3. Whisk the egg with the milk. Add to the flour and mix quickly to form a loose dough.
4. Turn the dough out onto a lightly floured work surface and knead gently until it comes together. Shape into a long rectangle 30cm wide by 20cm long.
5. Spread over the mincemeat, leaving a 3cm border all around the edges. Carefully roll the dough up like a Swiss roll, being careful not to compress it too much.
6. Cut the roll into 10 slices. Arrange the swirls side by side in the cake tin. Glaze with egg wash and scatter the top with flaked almonds. Bake for 25-30 minutes, until golden and risen. Leave to rest in the tin for 5 minutes before turning out onto a wire rack to cool. Dust with icing sugar to serve.

BAGELS

MAKES 9 BAGELS

I'd always wanted to make bagels but thought that they might be too much hassle. They're actually so easy to make and taste amazing, a great thing to make regularly at the weekend. When I was taking the photos for this recipe I halved the bagel, toasted it, covered it in cream cheese and made some coffee. Without even thinking I sat down and ate the bagel, forgetting to take the photo! They're that good - they'll make you forget what you're supposed to be doing and concentrate on the gorgeous chewy crust and cold cream cheese instead! To make cinnamon raisin bagels, just add 1 teaspoon cinnamon and 100g raisins to the dough.

300ml warm water
1 x 7g sachet fast-action yeast
½ tsp salt
pinch of caster sugar
580g strong white flour
2 tbsp sunflower oil
1 egg, beaten
sesame seeds
poppy seeds

1   Mix the water, yeast, salt and sugar together in a large bowl.
2   Add the flour and oil. Mix together until a dough forms, then knead for 10 minutes.
3   Divide the dough into 9 equal pieces. Make each ball of dough into a bun. Using your thumb, make a hole in the middle and gently rotate to form a bagel shape.
4   Place the bagels on 2 oiled baking trays. Leave to rise for 50 minutes in a warm, draught-free place covered with a clean tea towel, or until doubled in size.
5   Preheat the oven to 180°C. Grease 2 baking trays and bring a large pot of water to the boil.
6   Gently drop each bagel into the water. Turn them over every minute or so. After 3 minutes of boiling, carefully place each bagel on a rack to dry slightly.
7   Place the boiled bagels on the greased baking trays and glaze with the beaten egg. Sprinkle with the seeds.
8   Bake for 15 minutes, then turn over and bake for a further 5 minutes, until golden.

GUINNESS AND RYE BREAD

MAKES 1 LOAF

If you love the distinctive taste of stout, then this bread is for you! It's gorgeous with a strong cheddar cheese and some homemade chutney.

400g plain flour
170g rye flour
4 tsp baking powder
1 tbsp caster sugar
60g butter, cubed
1 x 330ml bottle of Guinness/stout

1   Preheat the oven to 210°C. Butter and flour a 1lb loaf tin.

2   Put the flours, baking powder and sugar into a bowl. Rub in the butter with your fingertips until the mixture resembles breadcrumbs.

3   Add the stout and stir to combine. Knead to a smooth dough for 2 minutes, either by hand or using the dough hook on your mixer.

4   Shape into a loaf and place in the tin. Cut a few lines over the top of the loaf.

5   Bake at 210°C for the first 10 minutes, then reduce the temperature to 180°C and bake for a further 50 minutes, until the loaf sounds hollow when you tap the base.

HONEY OAT BREAD

MAKES 1 LOAF

This is beautifully sweet, wholesome bread. It really does vary in flavour depending on what honey you use. My sister Ettie lives in Africa and brought home some Somali honey for my beekeeping father to try. The honey was dark and treacly with a strong smoky flavour and was really gorgeous in this bread. I wouldn't use expensive manuka honey, as the benefits of manuka will not survive the heat of the oven.

100g porridge oats
90g honey
25g butter, cubed
300ml boiling water
230g wholewheat flour
90g plain flour
1 x 7g sachet fast-action yeast

1 Put the oats, honey, butter and boiling water in a bowl. Stir and leave to cool down until it's lukewarm.

2 Mix the flours and yeast with the oat mixture. Knead until the dough is soft and pliable.

3 Place the dough in an oiled bowl and cover with a clean tea towel. Leave to rise in a warm, draught-free place for 1 hour, or until the dough has doubled in size.

4 Oil a 2lb loaf tin or a shallow sandwich tin. Knock back the dough by kneading and shaping the dough into a log or round and place it into the tin. Cover and leave to rise again for another hour or so, until risen.

5 Preheat the oven to 180°C.

6 Bake for 45 minutes, or until the bread sounds hollow when you tap the base.

SPICED SULTANA BREAD

MAKES 1 LOAF

....

This bread is so easy - you simply mix everything together and bake it!
It's one of those gorgeous recipes that makes the whole house smell
amazing and you will feel quite smug until you realise that the only one
in the kitchen to witness your culinary genius is the dog, and she's
been lulled to sleep by the humming oven and the comforting wafts of
cinnamon.

130g wholemeal flour
50g plain flour
75g Demerara sugar
1 tbsp baking powder
1 tsp cinnamon or mixed spice
pinch of salt
1 egg
225ml milk
75ml sunflower oil
1 tsp vanilla essence
100g sultanas

1 Preheat the oven to 180°C. Grease and flour a 1lb loaf tin.

2 Place the flours, sugar, baking powder, cinnamon and a pinch of salt into a large bowl.

3 Beat the egg in a jug, then add the milk, oil and vanilla.

4 Make a well in the centre of the dry ingredients and pour in the liquid. Stir with a wooden
   spoon until just combined, then stir through the sultanas.

5 Transfer the dough into the tin and bake for 35-40 minutes.

SEED LOAF

MAKES 1 LOAF

I love bread with loads of seeds and 'bits' in it! I always ate white bread when I was small, but it just doesn't fill me up any more. I love this bread toasted with honey or used to make an apple and cheese sandwich.

500g wholemeal bread flour
1 x 7g sachet fast-action yeast
1 tsp caster sugar
325ml warm water
1 tbsp vegetable oil
50g sunflower seeds
25g sesame seeds
25g linseeds
25g poppy seeds

1 Oil a 2lb loaf tin.
2 Mix the flour, yeast and sugar in a large bowl. Mix the water into the flour until a craggy dough is formed. Add the oil and knead on a lightly floured surface until smooth.
3 Gradually knead in all of the seeds until the dough is smooth and pliable. Shape into a loaf and place in the tin. Leave to rise for 30 minutes in a warm, draught-free place covered loosely with a clean tea towel.
4 Preheat the oven to 200°C.
5 Bake for 35–40 minutes. Remove from the tin for the final 5 minutes of baking, until the loaf sounds hollow when you tap the base.

HEALTH LOAF

MAKES 1 LOAF

I'm one of those people that love white crusty bread. It's addictive to me, so I usually steer clear of it because it's a slippery slope. The last time I overdosed on the white stuff was a Saturday morning in 1993 watching *Murder She Wrote* in my pyjamas. I ate seven slices of white toast with honey and butter and I couldn't even remember who the murderer was or how Jessica finally solved the case. Never again. Now I stick to brown bread, and the more seeds and bits in it, the better! This is a really easy, quick yeast-free bread that will sit happily in the bread bin all week. Gorgeous with a boiled egg or some bitter orange marmalade.

150g wholemeal flour
50g plain flour
50g chopped nuts (Brazil, pecan, hazelnuts, almonds)
50g linseeds
50g sunflower seeds
50g sesame seeds
1 tsp baking powder
1 tsp bread soda
½ tsp salt
1 egg
225ml buttermilk
75ml sunflower oil

1   Preheat the oven to 180°C. Grease and flour a 1lb loaf tin.
2   Place the flours, nuts, seeds, baking powder, bread soda and salt into a large bowl and stir to combine.
3   Beat the egg in a jug. Add the buttermilk and oil.
4   Make a well in the centre of the dry ingredients and pour in the liquid. Stir with a wooden spoon or your hand until just combined.
5   Transfer the dough into the tin. Bake for 50–60 minutes, until the loaf will happily come out of the tin.

ICED BUNS

MAKES 8 BUNS

Traditionally, the soft iced buns with raspberry jam have pink icing and the plain have white. This bun dough is very easy to make. All it needs is some time and warmth. The sweet smell of these buns baking is amazing – there's something about milk-based yeast dough that is very homely, probably because you can't really leave the house as you're waiting to reshape them after they double in size! Perfect for weekend baking. Be careful not to overfill the buns with jam.

FOR THE BUNS:
450g strong white flour
1 tbsp caster sugar
50g butter, softened
1 x 7g sachet fast-action yeast
275ml lukewarm milk
1 tsp vanilla essence
milk, for brushing

FOR THE ICING:
225g icing sugar, sieved
2-3 tbsp boiling water
a few drops of red food colouring

1 Mix the flour and sugar in a bowl. Rub in the butter with your fingertips until the mixture resembles breadcrumbs.

2 Mix the yeast with the warm milk and vanilla. Add the milk mixture to the flour.

3 Mix together in the bowl until a soft dough forms, then turn out and knead on a lightly floured surface for 8-10 minutes, until the dough is smooth and elastic.

4 Place the dough in an oiled bowl, cover with a clean tea towel and leave in a warm, draught-free place to rise for 1 hour, or until doubled in size.

5 Knock the dough back, divide into 8 pieces and shape into rectangles. Flatten each rectangle of dough and spread 1 teaspoon of jam onto one half of the dough. Carefully fold the dough over to keep the jam inside and form a roll.

6 Place the rolls on a floured baking tray and cover loosely with a clean tea towel. Leave to rise for another 20 minutes, until the buns have puffed up.

7 Preheat the oven to 200°C.

8 Brush the rolls gently with milk. Bake for 20-25 minutes, until golden. Carefully transfer the buns to a rack to cool completely.

9 Meanwhile, mix all the icing ingredients together. Add the food colouring sparingly – often one drop is enough.

10 Ice the cooled buns generously and leave to set on a wire rack. These are best eaten on the day they are made, but can be kept in an airtight tin for a day or two.

CHAPTER 6

Thrift

TIFFIN

MAKES 15-20 SLICES

This is one of the easiest things ever to make and requires no baking, yet everyone absolutely loves tiffin! This recipe is gorgeous and a tin full of tiffin makes a really nice present. We used to always be allowed to make this when we were small with the leftover biscuits from Christmas. A word of warning though: ginger is dominant, so if you want to use Ginger Nuts, go the whole hog and add bits of crystallised stem ginger to the mixture too. Also, shortbread tastes a bit horrible in tiffin, so maybe just throw that outside for the birds!

200g dark chocolate, chopped
150g butter
2 tbsp golden syrup
300g biscuits (digestives, Rich Tea, Polo, fruit shortcake, etc.)
200g sultanas
100g nuts, toasted and chopped

1. Line a square 25cm x 25cm tin with greaseproof paper.
2. Melt the chocolate, butter and golden syrup together in a heatproof bowl set over a bowl of simmering water. Stir occasionally to make sure everything is melting evenly.
3. Break the biscuits into bite-sized pieces and place in a large bowl. Don't worry if some bits are big, as they'll break down when you're stirring. Add the sultanas and nuts and combine well.
4. Pour the melted chocolate mixture over the biscuits and stir everything well to combine. Spoon into the tin. Compress and flatten the mixture with the back of the spoon.
5. Leave to set in a cold room or the fridge before cutting into bars.

CHESTER CAKE

MAKES 16 SLICES

I love this stuff! Chester cake is also known as gur cake and was made by bakeries to use up their stale bread. It could be bought cheaply by kids that had skipped school and it would keep them going until dinnertime! My mother makes the best Chester cake and very kindly rang me at the last minute to let me in on her secret ingredient: 2 tablespoons of marmalade. I was delighted that she had shared it with me and I made the cake, but it just wasn't the same. It was only then that she revealed her second tip: lemon juice in the icing. Finally, I have it perfected!

I like to use different teas when I'm soaking the bread; Earl Grey, chai and cinnamon and liquorice all work really well.

340g good-quality stale white bread
1 pot of strong, cold tea (chai, Earl Grey or normal)
90g plain flour
2 tbsp mixed spice
1 tsp baking powder
225g light brown sugar
60g butter
225g sultanas
2 eggs
120ml milk
2 tbsp marmalade
450g shortcrust pastry (see p. 115)

FOR THE ICING:
juice of 1 lemon
200g icing sugar, sieved

1 Cover the stale bread with the cold tea. Leave to soak for 1 hour.
2 Preheat the oven to 180°C. Butter a rectangular (20.5 cm x 32 cm) baking tin.
3 Squeeze the bread dry by pressing the mixture in a sieve over the sink. Transfer to a bowl and set aside.
4 Sieve the flour, mixed spice and baking powder into a bowl, then add the sugar. Rub in the butter with your fingertips until the mixture resembles breadcrumbs.
5 Add the sultanas to the bread and mix well, then add to the flour mixture and combine well.

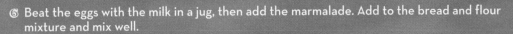

6 Beat the eggs with the milk in a jug, then add the marmalade. Add to the bread and flour mixture and mix well.

7 Roll out one half of the pastry to fit into the buttered baking tin. Prick the pastry base all over with a fork.

8 Spread the bread mixture over the pastry. Roll out the other half of the pastry, then cover the bread mixture with it and pinch the edges together to seal. Prick the top with a fork. Bake for 1 hour and 45 minutes, until golden. Cover loosely with foil if the pastry is browning too much. Leave to cool on a rack.

9 To make the icing, mix the lemon juice with the sugar until thick. Add more icing sugar or hot water depending on how thick the icing is. Spread generously over the cake and slice once set.

FRENCH TOAST

SERVES 2

French toast is the ultimate Sunday morning breakfast. I love dusting it with cinnamon sugar or maple syrup and slices of banana. My sister Daisy works at a bread stall in The English Market in Cork and she always says that challah, the sweet Jewish bread, makes the best French toast. She knows her stuff!

4 eggs
250ml milk
½ tsp vanilla essence
4 thick slices of day-old bread
1 tsp butter
sunflower oil, for frying
icing sugar, cinnamon and sugar or fruit compote, to serve

1 Whisk the eggs, milk and vanilla together, then pour into a shallow dish. Soak each slice of bread for 1 minute on each side in the eggy mixture.

2 Place a frying pan on a medium heat. Add the butter and a splash of sunflower oil. Gently fry the eggy bread, leaving each side to 'set' before flipping it over.

3 Remove the toast and place on a plate lined with kitchen paper. Keep in a warm place while you fry the remaining bread.

4 Dust with icing sugar or cinnamon and sugar and serve with fruit compote or a topping of your choice.

TRIFLE

SERVES 8

Trifle is an all-time favourite dessert, a classic comfort food. Every house should have a trifle bowl that gets brought out on a Sunday or at Christmas. I always use the Lemon Madeira (p. 38) as the base for my trifle. It adds a subtle flavour and there really is no beating a homemade cake base. It's worth freezing a few slices of leftover cake whenever you have it and then taking it out to make this gorgeous, thrifty trifle!

300g cake or half a Lemon Madeira (see p. 38)
500g frozen mixed berries
6 strawberries, sliced
110g caster sugar plus 2 tbsp
60g custard powder
450ml milk
150ml cream
1 egg yolk
1 tsp vanilla essence
250ml cream, whipped, to decorate
silver balls, to decorate (optional)

1 Slice the cake into fingers and arrange on the base of a large glass serving bowl.
2 Mix the frozen berries, strawberries and 2 tablespoons sugar together in a bowl, then spoon over the cake.
3 Combine the remaining 110g sugar and the custard powder in a pan. Stir in the milk and cream. Bring to the boil and keep stirring as it thickens. Remove from the heat and leave to cool slightly, then stir in the egg yolk and vanilla.
4 Pour the warm custard over the cake and berries. Smooth down the surface evenly. Cover with some greaseproof paper or cling film and place in the fridge until cold.
5 Once the custard is cold, remove the paper and top generously with the whipped cream. Scatter silver balls over and serve.

BROWN BETTY

SERVES 6–8

I have been known to buy breadcrumbs just to make this comforting dessert! Every time you have scraps of white bread, throw them in a bag in the freezer and then make breadcrumbs on a rainy day. It's a really quick and easy dish that is filling and warm on cold winter nights. It's also lovely made in individual ramekins and topped with cream, vanilla ice cream or custard.

4 eating apples (such as Cox Pippin or Golden Delicious)
3 cooking apples (such as Bramley)
40ml water
2 cloves
2 tbsp Demerara sugar
1½ tsp cinnamon, divided
75g butter
275g breadcrumbs
50g caster sugar
cream, vanilla ice cream or custard, to serve

1 Preheat the oven to 190°C. Butter an ovenproof dish.

2 Peel the apples and cut them into chunks. Place in a pan with the water and simmer for 10 minutes, until softened. Stir in the cloves, Demerara sugar and 1 teaspoon cinnamon with a wooden spoon. Keep stirring until most of the apple has broken down.

3 Meanwhile, melt the butter in a medium saucepan. Remove from the heat and stir in the breadcrumbs, mixing thoroughly. Add the caster sugar and the remaining $^1/_2$ teaspoon cinnamon.

4 Spread half the apple purée onto the base of the buttered ovenproof dish. Top with half of the breadcrumbs. Repeat with the remaining apple and breadcrumbs. Sprinkle the top with caster sugar and a few teaspoons of water. Bake for 30–40 minutes, until crisp. Serve warm with cream, ice cream or custard.

BREAD AND BUTTER PUDDING

SERVES 6-8

This is one of those nostalgic recipes that everyone loves. People always seem to have a secret ingredient - a tablespoon of marmalade, crystallised ginger, coffee liqueur or using brioche or challah as the base. I once read about a man who also spreads jam on his bread before layering the slices. I love the original too much to go messing around with it though!

500ml milk
1 vanilla pod
12 slices day-old bread
75g butter, softened
150g sultanas
4 eggs
65g caster sugar
200ml cream
Demerara sugar, for sprinkling

1   Place the milk in a saucepan. Cut the vanilla pod in half, scrape out the seeds and add to the milk, along with the pods. Gently heat the milk for 5 minutes, until it reaches body temperature.

2   Remove all the crusts from the bread and discard or keep for making breadcrumbs. Spread the bread liberally with butter and quarter each slice. Layer one-third of the bread in an ovenproof dish and sprinkle with one-third of the sultanas. Repeat twice, ending with a layer of sultanas.

3   Remove the vanilla pod from the milk. (You can rinse it and use it to make vanilla sugar.) Whisk the eggs in a jug, then pour over the warm milk while still whisking. Return the mixture to the saucepan, add the sugar and heat gently, whisking all the time, for 5 minutes. Remove from the heat and whisk in the cream.

4   Pour the custard over the bread slices. Sprinkle with Demerara sugar and leave to settle for at least 2 hours or overnight.

5   Preheat the oven to 180°C. Place the dish into a deep roasting pan onto the oven shelf. Pour hot water around the dish to come halfway up the sides. Bake for 40–50 minutes, until golden and set.

TIRAMISU

SERVES 8-10

This is another one of those 1970s desserts that everyone loves. I use leftover Marble Cake (see p. 32) for this as the chocolate goes well with it and the stale cake holds its shape and doesn't mush down. It's great for entertaining as you can make it the day before and serve it cold on its own, with fresh raspberries or just really good coffee.

500g mascarpone
55g icing sugar, sieved
200ml Baileys, divided
200ml cream
500ml really strong coffee
600g cake (I use the Marble Cake on p. 32)
2 chocolate Flake bars or 55g grated chocolate
cocoa powder, for dusting

1   Whisk the mascarpone with the sugar and 50ml Baileys until well combined. Add the cream and whisk until it has increased in volume and is soft.

2   Combine the coffee and the remaining 150ml Baileys in a shallow dish. Soak the fingers of cake in this mixture.

3   Place a single layer of the soaked cake on the base of a serving dish. Spread some cream mixture on top and crumble over some chocolate. Repeat twice, finishing with a layer of the mascarpone mixture. Leave to settle for a few hours or overnight. Dust generously with cocoa before serving.

PEACH AND RASPBERRY CRUMBLE

SERVES 6

I love crumbles. I always add oats and nuts, as they give a lovely texture as well as flavour. If you have any leftover Hazelnut Shortbread biscuits (see p. 98) you could crumble them into the mixture too. You can put any fruit in your crumble: apple, blackberry and a few sweet geranium leaves; rhubarb and vanilla; or plum and cardamom. I also like to make individual crumbles. You can make the topping and keep it in a Ziploc bag in the freezer for whenever you need a quick dessert. I nearly always make a big crumble like this for me and Colm and then end up eating it for breakfast the following morning with Greek yoghurt – so nice!

1 x 500g large tin of peaches or 4 fresh peaches
150g raspberries (frozen are fine)
60g whole almonds
100g plain flour
70g butter
60g caster sugar
35g porridge oats

1 Preheat the oven to 180°C.
2 Cut the peaches into thick slices and place in an ovenproof serving bowl along with the raspberries.
3 Blitz the whole almonds in a food processor until you are left with some ground almonds and some nibbed bits of nuts. Add the flour, butter, sugar and oats. Pulse until the mixture resembles breadcrumbs. Spread evenly over the fruit and bake for 30–40 minutes, until golden.

ETON MESS

SERVES 8-10

....

Eton Mess is quite simply an assembly job. This is what you make when someone hits off your swan masterpiece from p. 16 and it crashes all over the floor. Pick that meringue up, dust it off and make Eton Mess! The traditional recipe uses strawberries, but bananas, cream and caramel sauce is really lovely too, layered in a sundae glass.

1 large or 6 individual store-bought meringues or leftover meringue or pavlova
500ml cream, whipped
600g strawberries, sliced

▯ Break the meringues into large chunks. Gently fold all of the ingredients together in a large bowl until just combined – don't overmix. Serve in small glass bowls or ice cream sundae glasses.

QUEEN OF PUDDINGS

SERVES 8-10

This is the Queen of Puddings. Not just the Queen's best friend ever or the first cousin of the Queen - this *is* the Queen, so I had to make it. What a fine thing. Sponge bread, jam and meringue? Oh, you spoil me!

50g butter, softened
125g caster sugar, divided
600ml milk
zest of 1 lemon
150g breadcrumbs
4 large eggs, separated
4 tbsp raspberry jam

1 Preheat the oven to 180°C. Butter a 1-litre ovenproof dish or 4 x 300ml dishes.

2 Bring the butter, 25g sugar, the milk and lemon zest to a gentle simmer in a pan. Add the breadcrumbs and set aside, stirring often, until thickened. Stir the egg yolks into the mixture and spoon into the prepared dish. Bake for 15 minutes, or until just set. Set aside.

3 Meanwhile, heat the jam in a pan until it's runny. Carefully spread over the top of the pudding. Set aside.

4 Whisk the egg whites and the remaining 100g sugar in a spotlessly clean, dry bowl until soft peaks form.

5 Spoon or pipe the meringue over the top of the pudding and bake for 10 minutes, until the meringue is lightly browned and crisp. Serve immediately or while it's still warm, although it's nice cold too, with cream.

GOODY

SERVES 1

Goody is a typical thrifty Irish recipe. All of the ingredients are usually at home already and the resulting dish is warm, filling and comforting. You can use chunky white bread, challah, brioche or Spiced Sultana Bread (see p. 157) for this dish. This was traditionally made on Bonfire Night or Midsummer's Night, so next Bonfire Night make a big mug of goody to keep you warm and sit around the bonfire making sure the cat doesn't get too close to the flickering flames!

2 thick slices of white bread
150ml milk
handful of sultanas
1 tbsp caster sugar
pinch of mixed spice

1   Remove the crusts from the bread and cut each slice in half. Place the bread, milk and sultanas into a small saucepan. Heat gently and stir to break up some of the bread until the mixture is heated through. Stir through the sugar and spice.
2   Transfer to a small bowl or mug and eat with a spoon.

Happy Easter! xXx

CHAPTER 7

Must-Haves

VANILLA ESSENCE

MAKES 250ML

I always treat vanilla essence like liquid gold - a precious fragrant addition to any baked treat. My favourite vanilla essence is a dark umber flecked with black seeds. It transforms buttercream icings, brings cakes to life and is also extremely nice with roast duck. I buy my vanilla pods online, as they're much cheaper. In the supermarket they cost a fortune and you usually only get a couple of pods rattling round in a jar!

1 small jam jar
6 vanilla pods
250ml vodka, rum or brandy

1   First sterilise your jam jar by washing it well in hot, soapy water or in a dishwasher and then placing in a cold oven and slowly heating to 150°C. (Alternatively, you can place the jars in there when you're preheating the oven for something else.)
2   Slice each vanilla pod down the centre, but don't cut it in half fully. Curl each vanilla pod into the jam jar.
3   Next fill the jar with the alcohol of choice. Seal well with a lid and label it.
4   Keep in a cool, dark place for 8 weeks before using. Shake the jar every second day.
5   This will keep indefinitely as long as you top it up with more alcohol and add an extra bean every now and again.

COLOURED SUGAR

I'm not going to claim that making your own coloured sugar will save you thousands of euro a year, but it will brighten up sugar biscuits! Ice your St Patrick's Day shamrock cookies with white glacé icing and sprinkle with green sugar just before it sets - you can do the same for Valentine's Day love heart cookies or Halloween pumpkins to add a glittery sugary touch! It's a really easy 5-minute project that would make a lovely present for the baker in your life.

60g caster sugar
a few drops of food colouring

▢ Place the sugar in a jam jar or small lidded container. Add a few drops of food colouring. Tighten the lid and shake until the colour is evenly dispersed. Store in a cool, dark place.

VANILLA BUTTERCREAM

MAKES ENOUGH FOR 12 CUPCAKES OR TO FILL 1 LARGE CAKE

55g butter, softened
250g icing sugar, sieved
4 tbsp milk
1 tsp vanilla essence
1 drop of food colouring (optional)

Beat the butter with half the sugar in a bowl until light and fluffy. Add the remaining sugar and the milk, vanilla and food colouring, if using. The more you mix this, the fluffier and lighter the icing will become.

BERRY BUTTERCREAM

Fold 100g fresh berries, such as blueberries, raspberries or currants, through the vanilla buttercream.

CHOCOLATE BUTTERCREAM

MAKES ENOUGH FOR 12 CUPCAKES OR TO FILL 1 LARGE CAKE

55g butter, softened
230g icing sugar, sieved
40g cocoa powder, sieved
5 tbsp milk
½ tsp vanilla essence

Beat the butter with half the sugar in a bowl until light and fluffy. Add the remaining sugar and the cocoa, milk and vanilla. The more you mix this, the fluffier and lighter the icing will become.

Leabharlanna Poiblí Chathair Bhaile Átha Cliath
Dublin City Public Libraries

Index